to the
beginning
of the
end of

karma

Meetu Bisht

HAY HOUSE

Carlsbad, California • New York City
London • Sydney • New Delhi

Published in the United Kingdom by:
Hay House UK Ltd, 1st Floor, Crawford Corner,
91–93 Baker Street, London W1U 6QQ
Tel: +44 (0)20 3927 7290; www.hayhouse.co.uk

A catalogue record for this book is available from the British Library.

Tradepaper ISBN: 978-1-83782-671-1
E-book ISBN: 978-1-83782-672-8

10 9 8 7 6 5 4 3 2 1

This product uses responsibly sourced papers, including recycled materials and materials from other controlled sources. For more information, see www.hayhouse.co.uk

The authorized representative in the EU for product safety and compliance is Penguin Random House Ireland, Morrison Chambers, 32 Nassau Street, Dublin D02 YH68, Ireland. https://eu-contact.penguin.ie

Printed and bound by CPI Group (UK) Ltd, Croydon CR0 4YY

To the source energy—the Supreme Soul
whose love, inspiration, and guidance resulted in this effort.
I dedicate this book to you!

Contents

Section III
Karma: Course of Action

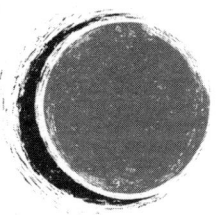

Introduction

We are all bound by an invisible contract with time, each of us experiencing a unique slice of our accumulated karmas—those ripe fruits of past actions now ready to be harvested. What propels us through this journey is a delicate interplay between our dominant tendencies and the karmic debts we carry. Together, they sculpt our experiences, carving out pathways for new learning and growth.

The purpose of life is to transform our life lessons into growth and evolve towards our higher self. However, our success in achieving this purpose depends solely on how well we understand karma and navigate it. Because despite being seen as the destroyer, karma is ultimately the enabler of our progress, which includes mental, emotional, material, and spiritual progress.

So, like everything else that is potentially life-changing and integral to human destiny, karma—its true meaning and purpose, its mechanisms and manifestations, the factors behind its creation, and the path to its resolution—demands deeper insight and clarity. This also means that one must reassess and redefine karma in a way that allows them to grasp their individual truth and take the necessary steps toward progress, rather than going in circles with complex inner and outer patterns, which only adds to their karmic burden.

This is the fundamental reason that inspired the creation of this book. It offers a renewed and practical approach to karma, guiding you towards the freedom, maturity, and growth that you seek. It delves into the depths and intricacies of karma and presents new and effective ways to overcome karmic challenges and resolve long-standing karmic cycles. And if you are ready to evolve, the book will choose you.

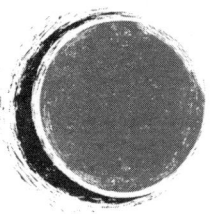

Prelude

The Tide Is Turning

From the recent developments and emerging insights, it has become evident that a new consciousness is gradually rising, and the winds of change are swiftly dismantling old perceptions, behaviours, and patterns to make way for something fresh, uncharted, and empowering. Never before have we witnessed such a surge in awareness and emphasis on mental, emotional, physical, and spiritual well-being. Humanity is investing unprecedented effort into understanding personal ignorance and egocentric behaviour. Wisdom is being shared on a global scale, fostering awareness of the dos and don'ts of life, and igniting new ideas about living more consciously. As a result, an increasing number of people are beginning to embrace life as a journey rather than a race. We are becoming more open to diverse life choices and better equipped to understand our reality. We are gradually embracing greater logic, common sense, and a more rational, pragmatic, sensitive, fair, and compassionate approach to life. We are beginning to challenge fears, question conventions, dismantle age-old belief systems, confront hierarchies, resist herd mentality, address gender disparities, and tackle corruption. We are striving to step beyond our limited selves, leave our comfort zones, and take responsibility for the damage caused in the past. At the same time, we are engaging in open conversations about mental health and the threats of climate change. There is a growing realisation among many of us about the mindless destruction and harm inflicted upon the planet, along with an awareness of the potential consequences that could lead to our own undoing.

This truly marks the beginning of the end of karma, both collective and individual. This is an opportunity to correct past mistakes and break the cycle of karma by embarking on a profound journey of transformation. And whether one embraces this shift or chooses to ignore it remains a personal choice, dictated by one's own sensibility and stage of evolution. But what is undeniably clear is that the present and future belong to a new consciousness and a new way of thinking, feeling, and being—a consciousness that is more compassionate and inclusive than discriminatory or selfish. This new consciousness is rounded, awakened, and wise, and it recognises ego as the true problem, rather than life, people, or circumstances. It seeks to look beyond superficial judgements, labels, and grievances, while encouraging self-examination for greater depth and maturity.

Moreover, at the root of this transformation is the desire to break free from a victim identity, helplessness, complaining, and the mental conditioning that has long trapped us in the illusion that life, people, and situations are responsible for our inner state. This transformation is driven by a willingness to unlearn depleting, limiting, and rigid concepts that have kept us clueless about how to move beyond fear, inaction, and a sense of entrapment. It stems from an openness to redefine key factors that shape who we are and how we live.

Among these factors, karma stands as the most dominant and daunting. It holds a powerful grip on both our imagination and our psyche. For centuries, humans have sought to decode karma, trying to understand its influence on the quality of life. Yet for just as long, karma has been feared, as our perception of it fuels victimhood, fear, confusion, and mystery.

However, with the rise of the new consciousness comes a willingness to move past this perplexing and anxious approach and embrace karma with courage, realism, and a commitment to course correction. The emphasis has shifted from philosophising karma to something actionable, effective, and empowering.

So, the big question now is: How do we move to the beginning of the end of karma? Are there clues in our ancient wisdom that we need to reinterpret in modern terms to work towards ending karma? Or are we already on that path, with destiny having taken over?

Ancient Wisdom in Action

In ancient Hindu mythology, there is a story about a major event called *samudra manthan*, which translates to 'churning of the ocean'. The story goes that when the forces of good (*devas* or divine beings) began to lose to the forces of evil (*asura* or demons), a higher consciousness intervened and guided the good towards a secret method to regain their lost powers. This method was the churning of the ocean, which eventually produced a magical nectar called *amrit*. Upon consuming this nectar, the lost powers of devas were restored, and good triumphed over evil.

This story holds even greater practical relevance and power in the present age, as some of us are ready for our own samudra manthan. Drawing on the practical and spiritual meaning of this term, it becomes clear that the real battle lies in overcoming our internal demons. As mentioned, samudra refers to the ocean, but in the context of spiritual growth and evolution, it symbolises the ocean of wisdom. The churning (manthan) represents the process of the human mind introspecting through this wisdom to release its inner poison (*vish*). Let's now look at how this aspect relates to karma.

Our karma creates emotions, emotions lead to suffering, and suffering produces poison. To rid ourselves of this poison, we must engage in the churning of wisdom—our own samudra manthan. Souls who reach this stage are blessed with amrit, the divine nectar of spiritual awakening and growth. Through this, lost powers are regained, and the greatest demon—our own ego—is overcome.

Thus, we can see that it is wisdom that serves as our ultimate tool for breaking karmic patterns. But this wisdom must be put into action, not left as mere words. And with the rise of a new consciousness, some of us are no longer intimidated by or captivated by fear-based ideas surrounding karma. Instead, we are taking proactive steps to address and resolve it ourselves. The focus is shifting from dwelling on what may have happened in the past or could happen in the future to what can be done in the present. This shift has been sparked by the realisation that we have allowed the ego to grow too powerful and destructive.

The surge of this new consciousness has opened deeper conversations around the ego, self-introspection, and self-realisation—conversations that were previously resisted as unnecessary. Now, there is a pressing need to reclaim lost powers and stop blaming external forces such as destiny, planets, karma, and even life itself for our mistakes and subsequent suffering. The big question, however, is—how do we regain our lost powers and reclaim control over our lives, something that is imperative to ending karma?

Restoration of Lost Powers

The journey to reclaim our lost powers begins with a process of unlearning and liberating ourselves from conceptual thinking, which is the playground of the ego. Until this happens, karma will likely remain a source of pain and mystery, causing guilt, dissatisfaction, disillusionment, and deception for many of us. The reason for this is that our conceptual thinking paints karma as the villain, blinding us to the bigger picture. As a result, karma remains a confusing and intimidating concept. This, in turn, leaves us unhealed, unhappy, and unsettled. Therefore, it is important to understand karma from a higher and deeper perspective so that we can transcend this fear. As the great Indian sage Paramhansa Yogananda said, 'Seeds of past karma cannot germinate if they are roasted in the fires of divine wisdom.' Put simply, turning wiser is the only path forward.

This book is an attempt not only to understand karma in its essence but also to explore the aspects that keep us trapped in a complex karmic matrix. By unravelling the true workings of karma, it highlights the positive aspects of even the most negative karma, which ultimately seeks the restoration of our higher self. The truth is that even the most negative karmic experiences are designed to guide us inward and help us resolve something deeper . . . something unhealed, unpleasant, and unresolved. Once we uncover these truths, we realise that karma is not a force to fear but a call to action—a chance to take back control of our spiritual journey.

This book is about reclaiming this control and freeing ourselves from the sense of victimisation or helplessness caused by perceived karmic influences. In fact, how we respond to karma can itself become a spiritual practice, and this book explores how to embrace this transformative approach.

Section I
Karma: Cause and Creation

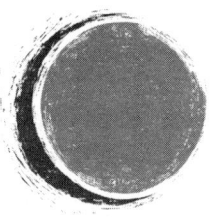

1

Why the Law of Karma?

Everything in the universe is in order. Nature follows this order. The sun, the moon, the stars, and the planets all maintain this harmony. Seasons come and go at their fixed times. They do what they are meant to, and unless man disrupts this harmony, nature rarely loses its balance.

What is important to notice here is that nothing in nature does more than what is necessary, and everything happens as it should. The plants, animals, and elements are all attuned to the rhythm of this order. They do not violate it. They take no more than what is necessary for survival. However, humans, despite the gift of intellect—which gives them the unique ability to think and act—tend to create disorder. They feed on nature and also take more than they need to satisfy their greed.

The truth is that human desires often exceed limits. A constant pursuit of sensory gratification, comfort, and pleasure leads humans to indulge in activities that disrupt the planet's natural balance and harmony, which are essential to sustaining this order. This balance and harmony are not confined to the physical elements or matter. They also depend on the planet's frequency and vibration which make up its overall energy. While elements and matter represent the surface reality (i.e., the forms), each of these forms, animate or inanimate, has a frequency and vibration that holds everything together. The planet itself is energy vibrating at a particular frequency.

And the continuity of life forms on the planet depends on maintaining the correct balance of this energy. Humans, like all living beings, are energy too, vibrating at their own unique frequencies. These frequencies combine to form the overall energy of the planet. Since humans depend on nature for survival, their energy impacts the energy of nature. When this energy is disturbed beyond a certain point, it manifests as natural calamities, threatening the survival of all life forms. As nature loses its purity due to an imbalanced and disempowering energy exchange with humans, disruption follows. And this disruption began when humanity lost its inner paradise to the ego due to excessive identification with form and a weakened spiritual connection. Over time, this disconnect caused a gradual shift in their energy field, lowering it to a frequency that was misaligned with nature's. Despite their capacity for intellect and reasoning, humans, driven by ego, began to disrupt nature's balance and peace. This growing imbalance not only affected the natural world but also began to distort humanity's perception of its own role in the larger ecosystem. It is also vital to understand that while intellect is a rare privilege and boon, the human mind, blinded by an indulgent ego, misinterpreted it as a sense of entitlement. This illusion of control over the forces of nature led to disorder, both within and all around. The ego inflated human pride and spurred destructive behaviour, eventually endangering the planet's energy and vitality.

But the cosmic intelligence—the source of all creation—far surpasses human intellect. This intelligence knows how to preserve order, restore balance, and prevent irreversible damage. It seeks to guide humanity back to its lost spiritual paradise and sanity by fostering realisation . . . a conscious awareness of their deeds, which is essential for correction and preservation. And in order to achieve this, the higher intelligence established a law to challenge the human ego by returning energy of the same quality, or heavier, as that sent out by ego-driven behaviour and actions. This law ensures that humanity experiences the consequences of its actions and energy and thereby is able to recognise what needs to be corrected to restore balance and harmony. This balancing force between order and disorder is called the law of karma.

The law of karma governs all aspects of human life to replace ego and ignorance with wisdom. It is neither a figment of imagination nor a derived theory. The law is real, and it functions with far greater efficiency than any human-made system. This law existed long before human intelligence comprehended or defined it, and it will continue to operate, regardless of doubt or disbelief.

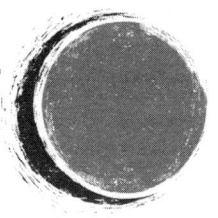

2

Past Lives and Karma

'Every man who, we think, gets something by chance, has been working for it slowly and surely through the ages.'
—Swami Vivekananda

Substantial research has been conducted on reincarnation, with numerous experiments providing evidence of past lives and their connection to the present. For those who don't believe in the possibility of past lives, they are free to hold that perspective. However, those who remain uncertain can explore the extensive body of evidence in the archives of past life research conducted by experts in psychoanalysis and past life regression. There is no need to elaborate further here, as ample factual, real-life evidence on the subject already exists.

Additionally, the truth about past lives can also be understood through present life experiences, particularly those of individuals who struggle to comprehend the reasons behind their circumstances. Many of us encounter experiences that seem to have no connection to who we are or the actions we take in our present lives. Haven't we all, at some point, heard people lament this perplexing contradiction? Or perhaps, we ourselves have faced situations where unexpected events unfolded, leading to unprecedented outcomes with no clear explanation for why they happened or why they continue to happen.

Here are some real-life grievances or complaints from people:

- 'I am good to everyone, but people are not nice to me.'
- 'I have always been a dutiful child, caring and loving, and have done more than I could for my parents. But they still favour my sibling, who cares little.'
- 'I have been very careful with money and investments, yet I became the victim of a scam and lost most of my savings.'
- 'That politician is corrupt and a troublemaker. Yet, he has never lost an election. Why do people keep voting for him?'
- 'He dropped out of school, has no job, yet drives an expensive car.'
- 'My brother is well-educated, kind, well-employed, and a good husband, but he still ended up in a messy divorce.'
- 'Despite being a consistent performer at work, I was handed a pink slip. Meanwhile, my non-

performing colleague with no merit was retained by the company.'

- 'He was involved in a fraud case, but he escaped punishment because he is rich.'
- 'I spent all my money on my children, and they abandoned me in my old age.'

These and many similar experiences seem to contradict the principle that people should receive outcomes aligned with their actions. So, why is it that sometimes people don't get what they deserve—or worse, get what they don't deserve? The answer lies in their past and what they bring into the present from their past.

What Is Karma?

In simple terms, karma is the energy of the deeds from our past lives that manifests as rewards or challenges in the present. And even though there are times when karma may knock on our doors much later—meaning after several lifetimes of those deeds—it never loses its address. No one is spared the consequences of their actions, as they are delivered at the right time by the law of karma, which restores justice and balance in the world. Therefore, the principle of rebirth aligns with the law of karma. Let us explore this further.

We are souls inhabiting human form. The soul is energy that gives life to the physical body. Energy drives the body and grants it the capability and power to think, feel, act, and create. This energy cannot be destroyed. So, when the form dissolves through death, the energy either remains in its original state, vibrating at the frequency of its tendencies, or it inhabits another form, experiencing life through ingrained tendencies. These tendencies provide vital proof of the reality of past lives.

Our thoughts and feelings arise from the psychological imprints or mental impressions stored in the subconscious, shaped by our past experiences. These subtle impressions reach the conscious level of the mind when a soul takes human form and engages with life, eventually revealing themselves through our tendencies. In ancient Hindu philosophy, these tendencies are referred to as *samskaras*. And since even infants display distinct tendencies, it suggests that these impressions are carried over from past lives. Additionally, the more dominant tendencies of a soul result from repeated thinking, feeling, and behaving in a certain way. Together, these become the soul's conditioning, which varies from soul to soul depending on its individual identification with certain thoughts, feelings, and emotions in response to life. Thus, how a soul has identified with and encountered life throughout its journey is of vital importance, and it engages with life through its tendencies.

What Are Tendencies?

As discussed, tendencies arise from identification with thoughts and feelings created by the soul as a response to life and its experiences. So, if a soul in its previous lifetimes identified with thoughts and feelings that are positive in nature and built a positive inner response to its outer life, it continues to vibrate at a positive frequency. This continues even after death, and when the soul begins its next journey in another form. However, if a soul was heavily identified with negative thoughts, feelings, and emotions during its past lives, it continues to vibrate at a negative frequency. This is why we find different people in the world with different dispositions, i.e., they have different responses to life, their environment, and experiences. Even infants respond differently to their environment due to their unique inherent tendencies. But how does this happen? Is it possible that the baby is conditioned in some way? How can a baby or child exhibit tendencies even before they have encountered life or had any significant experiences? Let us understand this through an example from my personal experience.

During an intercontinental trip, I once met a pair of twins, barely a year old, onboard a flight. They occupied seats ahead of me in the opposite row, and everything seemed fine in the initial few minutes as their parents settled in. The babies were endearing, and one felt drawn to them. The twins seemed happy and playful until one of them gradually started showing signs of discomfort and unrest. The gradual unrest soon turned to bawling, and to everyone's dismay, it continued for hours. Their parents tried every trick to pacify the baby and invoke a sense of calm. They took turns walking back and forth on the aisle with the baby, but all in vain. The baby's screams grew louder. The tension on the baby's face was palpable. Crying incessantly, his face had turned red. An hour passed like this until the baby was so tired that it fell asleep. The other twin, meanwhile, watched its sibling in wonder but seemed in no mood to join in.

Until the time the distressed baby was asleep, everything seemed normal. But the moment he woke up, his cries pierced through everyone's hearts and ears. There was unrelenting trauma that spoke through his sighs and screams. As co-passengers, we were equally worried. Then there was the other twin, still unaffected by all the crying and shouting around him. He remained active and vivacious. Thankfully, upon landing, everything eased, and once again, calmness prevailed.

What came as a strange coincidence, or shock, if I may use the word for better understanding, was that the same family of twins was onboard with us on our return journey. And what unfolded was familiar. The happy twin, again zen-like, remained at ease, while the one in deep turmoil cried at the top of his lungs for hours. It was clear the latter was unable to handle the environment of the flight. Though his sibling remained unruffled and poised, one wondered what kept one of them in such an intense state of anxiety and fear.

Quite clearly, a child is a child in its form identity. What is within that form is consciousness or energy, which feels something because fear has been triggered in its memory. This fear is a tendency. The child was responding to its environment based on this tendency, which evidently had remained unresolved and was part of its thoughts and feelings in a similar environment. The past was evident in the child's present, and this was the only logical link to why this child was so distressed on both occasions.

Therefore, our past, in the form of tendencies, stays in consciousness as it changes forms between life and death. What happened to the child—its experience while onboard the flight—was a return of energy that kept disturbing the child because there was something far deeper attached to its consciousness. Maybe in the past, this soul had a negative life experience onboard a flight, which conditioned it in a certain way towards the same environment. And thus, the moment this soul familiarised itself with the flight environment, what got triggered was extreme unrest. This did not happen with the other twin because it was not carrying negative baggage and had a lighter consciousness.

This example points to the reality of the past, and to understand karma, we must be able to comprehend the past. For we all respond differently to life situations because of this past. The important takeaway here is that the influence of our past can vary in degrees depending on our state of self-awareness, and even the most rigid tendencies, with all their negative influences, can be transformed. This is the very basis of karma correction because karma results from tendencies. And without understanding the nature and influence of our tendencies—what they attract in terms of energy, experiences, and life events—we cannot even begin to resolve karma.

In fact, our entire life revolves around either correcting or strengthening these tendencies, as they ultimately also take care of our karmic settlements. So, the circumstances we encounter, the families we are born into, our living environments, societies, and cultures are all conducive to our spiritual growth and karmic settlement, influenced by past life energy exchanges.

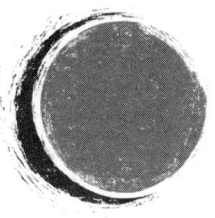

3

The Basis of Karma Creation

To truly understand karma, we must first examine its root. The image provided offers a simplified overview, which is further explained below.

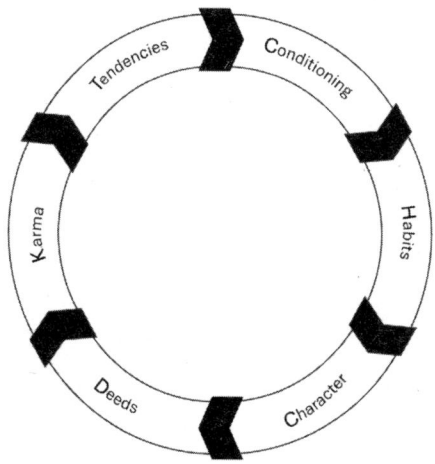

As covered in the previous chapter, our tendencies are shaped by our thoughts and feelings, as well as the actions we take based on them. So, for instance, if in their past lives, someone strongly identified with negative thoughts that invoked feelings of anger, and this anger led to actions intended to harm or seek revenge, those actions would imprint anger in their subconscious. This imprint would then manifest as a tendency. As a result, in their current life, even the slightest provocation could easily trigger anger in their behaviour, and they may also attract people with anger issues.

Similarly, if someone in their past repeatedly identified with positive thoughts and felt good, their actions would have been driven by an intention to do good for others. This would create a tendency for goodness or kindness, imprinted as a positive impression in their subconscious. As a result, this person would naturally exhibit kindness and goodwill towards others and would also attract the same.

So, tendencies are the seeds from which our conditioning grows. Over time, repeated tendencies become ingrained, forming habits that define our character—essentially, the soul's personality. Our tendencies vibe at a frequency, which can be categorised as either low or high, and our actions are shaped by the conditioning that arises from our tendencies. The more we identify with and act from our conditioning, the stronger our habits become, influencing whether we lean towards positive or negative behaviours that form character. A character formed by negative tendencies—unhealthy habits and behaviour—vibrates at a low frequency, while one shaped by positive tendencies and healthy habits vibrates at a higher frequency.

Moreover, the vibration of our character directly impacts the nature of our deeds. Our deeds are patterns of behaviour driven by our character, and these patterns carry the energy of karma. Since the soul itself is energy, the energy imprinted by karma stays with the soul in the state in which it was created, guiding the soul's journey over time. In other words, high-vibration deeds result in positive or good karma, while low-vibration deeds lead to the creation of negative or bad karma. Therefore, at the heart of every karma lies an underlying tendency, and our task is to identify these tendencies and dissolve them.

Let us now understand the influence of tendencies on karma through some examples.

- **Example 1: Tendency of Greed**

   Say we have a tendency towards greed, and each time we enter a negotiation over money, we demand a price which is much higher than what is fair and what we deserve. Sometimes we succeed in getting the sum, but at other times, we do not. This is when we can evaluate whether our demands are fair or if we can be more accommodating of the other person's capacity. However, if we remain adamant about our expectations, we change nothing. Even though we may lose many deals due to our inflexible approach, we remain convinced about what we believe we should get. Here, the dominant tendency of greed is being repeatedly used, and with its repetition, negative conditioning is formed because greed is a negative tendency. This conditioning reinforces the belief that 'we must have more'. The habit that arises from such conditioning is one of extracting more from others, which makes our behaviour greedy.

So, while greed may begin as a mere tendency, when it becomes habitual—when we exploit others to satisfy our greed—it manifests in our behaviour and reflects in our character. Karma is created when someone who cannot afford to meet our demands feels pressured to do so. Their resulting unrest and loss become the foundation of our gain, which qualifies as a low-vibration deed that generates low-vibration consequences with karma.

- **Example 2: Tendency of Attachment**

Now consider another scenario involving the tendency of attachment. If we often think excessively about the people we are close to or the things we possess, this attachment can lead to deriving our sense of self from people and possessions. Such dependence can result in obsessive thinking, which promotes negative conditioning based on the fear of losing what we hold dear. This can create habits of being over-possessive, controlling, or overly anxious. Such habits again give rise to a character with low vibrations and operating from such a character can create discomfort in relationships.

In the case of material possessions, we might be unwilling to share with others, which amounts to selfishness. Consequently, our deeds become low-vibration deeds. Thus, while attachment may be our tendency, when we repeatedly respond through it, it manifests in actions as selfishness, preventing us from sharing and leading to disputes over material things. If someone tries to take what we have, it may even provoke anger or violence. Similarly, in relationships, attachment can make us so controlling and possessive that others feel suffocated and disturbed. This is where our low-vibration deeds lead to the creation of low-vibration consequences with karma.

- **Example 3: Tendency of Peace**

When we repeatedly use the tendency of peace, regardless of how challenging the external situations in our lives are, we cultivate inner balance and strength. When we approach life from this place of inner balance and strength, we develop positive conditioning which enables us to accept and face life's challenges rather than waste time and energy resisting them. And as we use peace more often, we create the habit of staying calm. This habit leads to the formation of a peaceful character that emits high vibrations.

Additionally, deeds performed under the influence of peace are of high vibration. Such deeds comfort others, help find solutions to life's challenges, and sometimes even guide others to align with their own sense of peace, making them feel better. High-vibration deeds like these generate positive energy and high-vibration karma.

- **Example 4: Tendency of Happiness**

  When there is a tendency to stay happy, it keeps us light and instils a sense of vibrancy and vitality. This helps us remain in good spirits and enhances our productivity. With happiness, we uplift not just ourselves but also others and become less reactive to the negativity around us. Such positive conditioning nurtures a habit of being light-hearted and easygoing. Our character radiates high vibrations, and we remain sweet-tempered. Also, our good nature inspires high-vibration deeds, such as creating positive atmospheres wherever we go. Such deeds generate good energy with high-vibration karma.

The above examples reveal a fundamental truth: karma is not just a byproduct of our actions, but the direct result of our deeds. Deeds are patterns of behaviour that reflect our character or soul personality. In essence, we are the sum total of our deeds.

The consequences of our deeds return to us as karma, and the nature of these consequences determines the quality of our karma—something we will explore in the next chapter.

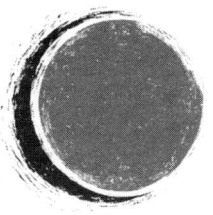

4

Cause and Effect in Karma

'Karma is the law of action or cosmic justice, based upon cause and effect.'
—**Paramhansa Yogananda**

Now that we have understood how tendencies relate to karma, let's discuss the finer details of what karma is and how it is created by applying the law of cause and effect.

At its core, karma is deeply intertwined with our soul's journey through the world of forms. Our body serves as our vehicle in this world of forms, while we are souls or energy beings in human form. It is also well-known that energy, once created, cannot be destroyed; it can only be transformed (law of conservation of energy). What drives this transformation is the soul's participation in the world of forms. This means that through its various births, a soul transforms in both positive and negative ways.

As explained in the previous chapter, souls possess a character or personality. They interact with the world of forms through this personality, which comprises soul tendencies, conditioning, habits, and character. This personality shapes how the soul thinks, feels, speaks, and acts, all of which carry energy. This energy helps the soul interact with the world. In human form, a soul exchanges energy with living beings (humans and nature) and reacts to non-living things (wealth, objects, places, etc.) in ways that generate a response to its own energy. This response leads to a new experience for the soul, to which it reacts through its personality. This reaction further shapes its personality and the situation, leading to consequences. The energy of these consequences returns to the soul as karma.

Thus, the way a soul engages in life—which, in Eastern philosophies, is described as *karm*—influences its immediate environment, the people it interacts with, and its own inner environment or soul personality. Karm encompasses a soul's thoughts, feelings, intentions, and actions. These elements not only influence but also evoke a response from both the animate and inanimate worlds, and this response generates new energy. So, karma creation depends on how the soul processes this energy.

At the root of karma is the soul's karm—its inherent personality—and the way this personality interacts with the world of forms. Karm is the true cause that sets an effect in motion, and depending on the quality of this effect, a specific type of karma is created.

According to the law of cause and effect, every event has a cause, and every effect has consequences. Let us apply this to understand karma creation. The response to the soul's interactions with the world depends on its own energy or karm. As the karm, so is the outcome of this interaction. The interaction itself is an event, and its outcome is determined by a cause—the soul's personality, energy, or karm. How the soul further responds to this event creates an effect, leaving an impression on its personality. This impression becomes karma.

Karma, however, is more than just action and reaction. The universal law of cause and effect, in the context of karma, requires deeper analysis. Let us consider an example:

Brian is a bitter man who often abuses others. His soul personality interacts negatively with the world—this is his karm. Brian's interactions provoke negative responses from others, and in one such instance, he is physically assaulted. This is the response to Brian's actions (or karm). The event has a cause—Brian's behaviour and personality—which generates new energy. It also triggers a response in Brian, leading him to further action. His reaction creates an effect, leaving an impression that results in karma. Now, consider three possible scenarios:

1. **High-intensity negative karma:** If Brian reacts with further negativity—attacking the offender and retaliating—he reinforces both his own negativity and that of the situation. This intensifies the effect, leading to severe karmic consequences.

2. **Low-intensity negative karma:** If Brian refrains from reacting negatively, perhaps due to others intervening and diffusing the situation, the effect does not carry severe consequences. However, it still generates low-intensity negative karma because Brian has neither transformed the energy of the interaction nor changed his own energy.

3. **Transformation and positive karma:** If Brian immediately realises his wrongdoing and tenders an apology—either on his own or after others intervene—this shifts the energy of the situation. His realisation and change in attitude not only transform a negative event but also his own energy. Such an effect has positive consequences.

Let us take another example related to parenting to understand cause and effect.

Say a parent operates through a soul personality that is highly suspicious and, as a result, curbs their child's freedom. This leads to the child losing self-confidence. The parent's behaviour and approach to parenting constitute their karm, which causes the event—the child's loss of confidence. The cause of this event is the parent's behaviour or karm. The event triggers a response, which creates an effect. How the parent responds to their child's loss of confidence determines the effect, which in turn has consequences that return as karma.

If the parent remains insensitive, does nothing to rebuild their child's confidence, and further blames the child for being unworthy, their response shows no transformation of energy. Instead, it amplifies negativity, leading to worse consequences and high-intensity negative karma. However, if the parent understands what went wrong and acknowledges their mistake, their response has a neutral effect and does not create severe consequences. But because they do not actively transform their child's life or their own behaviour, the possibility of karma creation remains. On the other hand, if the parent, after realising their mistake, gains deeper insight and takes appropriate steps to restore their child's confidence, their response has a positive effect with positive consequences, resulting in good karma.

Therefore, based on these examples, we understand that karma is defined by both an attribute and an intensity. This intensity can be further categorised into three qualities:

1. High-intensity negative
2. Low-intensity negative
3. Positive (which can also vary in degrees)

The third quality emerges from self-realisation and appropriate, timely action, which involves the transformation of negative energy into positive. The second quality depends on the level of acceptance and mental response, while the first results from a lack of realisation and inaction on the part of the doer.

The important point to note here is that the law of cause and effect is precise and repeats the cause over lifetimes until the right effect is created through the soul's own realisation. This law does not allow us to bypass learning or avoid the shift in consciousness. It recreates similar external events and experiences in different ways across lifetimes until the necessary shift in consciousness occurs. This is why it is said that energy, once created, cannot be destroyed; it can only be transformed. This understanding also brings clarity to those who think of karma as a form of punishment. In reality, karma is an opportunity to learn, develop higher self-awareness, and return to a more empowered inner state. This movement from ignorance to self-realisation is the ultimate purpose of the law of karma.

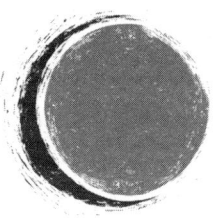

5

Simplifying Karma

Once we understand the basis of karma creation, we realise that karma is much more than just give and take. It isn't merely the exchange of energy with other aspects of human life but also the purification of the soul through such an exchange. As long as a particular cycle of karma continues for a soul, it reincarnates into another form, another life, to fulfil its unfinished tasks. These tasks are shaped by three key factors:

1. The energy created by a soul's deeds and the consequences of those deeds.

2. The return energy, which is experienced as either a debt to be repaid or a reward to be received.

3. The tendencies embedded in the soul's character that require change or reinforcement. These tendencies influence karmic outcomes and must be addressed to elevate the soul's consciousness.

Together, these factors form what we commonly understand as fate or a soul contract. This contract is tied to time, allowing us to free ourselves from a certain portion of our karmic burden while learning and evolving through our experiences. The most vital component of fate is karma. It is often believed that unresolved karma binds the soul to the cycle of life and death, compelling it to return until balance is achieved. In essence, karma functions as a ledger of unresolved energy and exchanges—a system of give-and-take to be completed. A soul is drawn back to repay its debts, fulfil obligations, or receive its dues from others in order to complete the spiritual transactions necessary for growth and evolution. However, the physical exchange is only a small component of karma, as karma holds a much deeper meaning and purpose. Let's explore this in more detail.

While it is true that a pending exchange of energy is the reason a soul is reborn, karma is not just about payback or repayment. The exchange is the interaction of a soul with life or others through thoughts, feelings, intentions, and actions. But karma is also what occurs after this exchange. Meaning, it also relates to the energy a soul creates in response to its interaction with other life forms. And the inability to give the right response creates bad karma, while the wisdom to respond appropriately to a challenging situation leads to the cancellation of old karmic debts.

The important takeaway here is that what remains within one's control is the transformation of the energy of karma through self-realisation. We can transcend the influence of this energy and create no further energy that would return to us as karma. However, this requires enlightenment and the dissolution of the ego. When the ego dissolves, one begins to respond to karma in ways that no longer accumulate further karmic debts. To reach such a state, a soul must first transform the energy of its pending karmic debts. This transformation begins with changes in the soul's conditioning, habits, tendencies, and character. Furthermore, since the soul is energy, the energy of its karma remains with it in the same state in which it was created. It is stored in the subconscious as the soul's subtle memory and manifests through its tendencies. The following example illustrates this aspect.

Person A is in a complicated relationship with person B, who is emotionally and verbally abusive toward them. In this dynamic, the abuse serves as the interaction or exchange of energy. As a result, person A silently suffers, which eventually becomes the cause of their depression.

The key point here is how person A handles this inner turmoil and what actions they take in response—this constitutes the effect and its consequences, resulting in either good or bad karma. If they continue to endure the abuse and suffer silently, the effect will manifest as a victim identity. This identity gives rise to a tendency of anger, which becomes imprinted in their soul memory. Over time, this anger will also attract more anger from person B, as they unconsciously feed off the energy field created by person A's unaddressed emotions. Even if this anger does not directly surface as aggression, it remains present as energy. And souls communicate through energy, which explains why we can sense something about each other without words, or even despite physical distance. So, when their anger is left unresolved, it becomes ingrained as a tendency in both person A and B. This shared tendency shapes their perspectives and reactions, eventually forming a habit. Over time, this habit moulds their character and behaviour, making anger a dominant part of their personalities.

What occurred between person A and person B was an exchange of energy. However, their individual responses to this exchange determine their karma. What remains in their soul memory is not the specific situation, but the unresolved anger. While the details of the situation will fade once they move beyond their current physical forms, the imprint of anger will persist. This imprint is their karma—something they will need to address and resolve, either in the present or in future lifetimes, as it will continue to draw similar patterns of anger into their relationships. If the same anger is observed and some action is taken to dissolve it, then there would be no pending karma. The release of this anger and the healing of these souls will result in peace, forgiveness, and letting go. This will make the energy exchange lighter and strengthen their soul personality, amounting to the transformation of energy—the precondition of the law of karma that helps end karmic debts. However, if anger remains, they will continue to act on this tendency, accumulating more karma through different life situations that may push them into further discomfort. As a result, their suffering will increase, eventually leading to awareness of their inner state, as the main purpose of suffering is to create higher self-awareness. The same unaddressed anger can also remain in these souls for multiple lifetimes, and they will continue to use it, making the tendency self-destructive. This is often the case with criminals and even people who end up causing self-harm.

Overall, it is our ignorance that makes us feel like victims of situations and circumstances, where we believe life is happening to us in a certain way. We think we are being made angry by an external stimulus and fail to realise that anger is our acquired tendency being actively used by us. And though we have the free will to not use what harms us, we are conditioned to believe that life makes us behave a certain way and that we have no choice or freedom to choose to be someone different. As a result, we give up. And this is when extreme steps are taken.

So, when a tendency reaches the peak of destruction, a soul earns a life where resolving this tendency becomes its primary mandate. This mandate is the key aspect of what is also called *prarabdha* karma—the karma one must experience. And for different people, there is a different prarabdha. It all depends on the maturity of their karma, which returns as a life situation, experience, and tendency that must be resolved because it has reached the peak of destruction.

In the above example, person A and person B may or may not essentially meet again, but they will need to go through relationships and life situations that will reflect the anger within them, thus pushing them towards understanding themselves and correcting the karma at a deeper level.

Here we need to understand that we attract what we are. Our own subjective reality or energy gets reflected in life situations and in our relationships with others. Life, in itself, does nothing; it only returns what has been created and has remained with the soul as a tendency. The dissolving or strengthening of this tendency, depending on how depleting or energising it is for the soul, is also pending karma. In simple terms, it is tendencies that create karma, and tendencies that end it. So, if one uses peace as a habit more than anger, they become peaceful, which becomes their character. And as the vibration of one's character is, so are their deeds. Deeds, as mentioned earlier, are the patterns that our character weaves, and it is these patterns that hold the energy of karma.

Thus, we can see that someone who is peaceful will quite clearly create good karma. But the question that arises is: what is the karmic mandate for such a person in their life? Their karmic mandate is to be a peacekeeper. For such souls, the mandate is to create more peace and harmony, serving as a balancing vibrational force on the planet. These souls, through their peaceful character and vibe, can help more unconscious, peaceless beings understand peace and elevate their consciousness to vibrate at the frequency of peace.

This underscores the fact that our karmic mandate is much deeper than our conceptual thinking and understanding of it. We can say that karma stays in the sands of time as one's footprints or energy field. When one returns, they catch the trail of their own footprints once again, to finish what was left unfinished or to address what remained as a burden in the subconscious memory. Therefore, if we choose to live consciously today, we can ensure that the walk to our destination gets easier—not just for now, but also the next time we are here. Or we can ensure that the trail isn't confusing and we never lose our way. So, our karma is in our hands. Remember, karma isn't going anywhere. You may eventually leave your physical form, but the karma you leave behind will decide the course of your journey when you are back. It will also set a mandate, which you will have to honour.

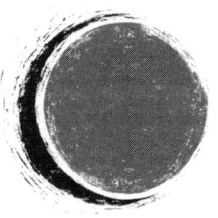

6

Tendency: The Seed of Karma

'The results of actions are impermanent and pass away. Yet, their seeds form an ocean of karma which becomes a barrier to a seeker's progress.'
—Ramana Maharshi

There is so much that contributes to the creation of karma, yet everything about karma starts and ends with a tendency and one's behaviour. So, even if we consider karma as pure give-and-take or payback, it doesn't conclude with the end of an event or experience connected to the exchange. The physical exchange through actions or emotions does not close karmic chapters altogether. This means that if one person cheats another, and the other person either walks out on them or cheats them in return, the two remain karmically connected until one or both realise that betrayal (cheating) or anger (walking out) must be replaced with a more harmonious and positive resolution.

In other words, the wrongdoer must deeply realise what is wrong in their actions and behaviour, accept their mistake, and offer a sincere apology without repeating the same behaviour. And even if the person who was cheated decides they no longer wish to continue the relationship, their karmic connection ends only when they fully accept the situation as it is—without wishing it to be something else. Because, especially in a negative situation, when one wants things to be different from what they are, it gives rise to anger, hate, animosity, and a sense of betrayal. So, if the one who has been betrayed decides to either stay in the equation or leave without creating or holding any negativity in their thoughts, feelings, or emotions, their karma reaches closure, as they have successfully moved the relationship to a more positive orbit. And this is because they have let go of anger and transformed the energy. Thus, we can conclude that karma only dissolves when the seed is corrected, and the seed in every karma is our tendency.

But why is tendency so important? Why is it the seed of karma? It is because a soul does not achieve spiritual growth, liberation, or even peace merely by the ending of the karmic exchange or an event that involves karmic payback. This happens because any karmic exchange has two sides: visible karma and invisible karma. Let's explore these in greater detail.

Visible karma is the event that occurs as per the law of karma, which mandates that any wrongful act committed against someone must be repaid to the

wrongdoer in equal or greater measure. Similarly, anything wrongfully taken from someone must be returned to the wronged individual by the wrongdoer in equal or greater degree. Thus, there is retribution, and the law delivers justice.

But this is only the tip of the iceberg because what we see and think of as karma in terms of an event or experience is much smaller than what karma truly is. The real part of karma is submerged in the ocean of ignorance and ego, and one is only able to grasp it through self-realisation, which arises from the awakening of consciousness. This often happens through some form of extreme suffering, as it removes the veil of ignorance and cracks the ego. And as the light of wisdom and realisation enters the soul, it prevents further harm that a negative tendency could cause, thus putting an end to karmic misery by setting the individual on the path of course correction.

So, what invisible karma mandates is one's growth by breaking free from the harmful effects of negative tendencies. To achieve this mandate, one needs to:

- Look within and become self-aware.
- Identify the negative tendencies that have caused the adverse events leading to spiritual decline and suffering.
- Seek liberation from damaging tendencies.

And so, unless one arrives at a place of deep realisation about their own ignorance and begins working toward freedom from a negative tendency, peace and happiness remain elusive. Both peace and happiness are high-vibration tendencies that can only be accessed by shifting consciousness to a higher frequency. This shift allows the soul to vibrate at a frequency higher than the one at which negative karma was created.

Let us understand this through an example with two fictional characters, Sam and Peter.

Sam and Peter are friends, and Sam owes some money to Peter. However, as greed takes over, he decides not to return it even when he is able to. This angers Peter, who chooses to cut ties with his friend.

Sam, therefore, retains greed over friendship, while Peter retains anger. So, the invisible karma for Sam is the dissolution of greed, and for Peter, the dissolution of anger. However, these souls continue operating at the frequency of greed and anger, and even when they return in another form in another life, Sam, out of greed, will deceive many more people, and Peter, out of anger, will struggle to trust anyone. The law of karma will ensure that they meet again, but if they have transcended their old forms and taken new births, Sam and Peter may not recognise each other. However, they will meet through a new relationship or even as strangers because the law of karma will not spare Sam from returning Peter's money. Additionally, their past exchange would remain in their soul memory as a subtle feeling or as energy, and it will only add a stronger force to their tendencies. Therefore, it is likely that when they encounter each other in their new forms, a highly negative situation will unfold.

The same could have been avoided or its magnitude reduced if Sam had been regretful and apologetic for his failure to return Peter's money and had stopped being greedy after that one odd episode. Or if Peter had not accumulated anger and doubt and had continued trusting others. This way, they both would have moved to a higher frequency than that of the original event, which would have helped them avoid further damage of higher intensity. But since they both remained ignorant of what was within and reacted to their external situations through an internal trait that was more damaging, Sam and Peter continued weaving patterns of anger and greed. Therefore, their next encounter is bound to be intensely negative.

So, we can see that the law of karma operates on similar lines as the law of the land. Just as one takes a loan from a bank and returns it with interest, what one owes to someone under the law of karma must be returned with interest. Another important fact is that we all have invisible karma, which keeps bringing us back into the cycle of life and death. But ironically, we only pay attention to the visible karma, and so our concepts of karma refer only to the tip of the iceberg. Thus, peace and freedom remain elusive, and we continue our journey in this world of forms, holding life and people responsible for all the wrongs that happen to us. Not realising that it is the negative tendency—the forbidden fruit—that, once tasted, can become the cause of one's fall from grace (spiritual nature). And when tasted (used) repeatedly, the same tendency can convert our inner paradise into a living hell, creating a heavier burden of karma. This is invisible karma, the hidden and heavier part of the iceberg.

If unresolved for long, invisible karma becomes more menacing and manifests in increasingly threatening ways over time, causing visible karma to escalate as well. Therefore, across different lifetimes, Sam and Peter, with greed and anger respectively, will continue to accumulate negative karma through negative deeds stemming from their unresolved tendencies. Because when greed is indulged for too long, it can turn someone into a scamster. And so, at some point, Sam will have to endure strict legal action. This could mean long-term imprisonment, heavy penalties, and excessive suffering—which, at that stage of his evolutionary journey, will be his prarabdha karma, the karma he must confront. His punishment may be so severe that his eventual suffering could lead to self-realisation and an understanding of greed, which he will only recognise as self-destructive at that point.

In the case of Peter, long-term anger can convert into cynicism, doubt, and a revenge mindset. He can attack, rob, and harm someone and it could be Sam, because the law of karma, as it takes its course, will bring them together to settle scores. Since both Sam and Peter remain ignorant of their tendencies, the nature of such a settlement would be unpleasant and ugly. But for them to come face to face and reach such a transformative stage where they end both visible and invisible karma could take several lifetimes from where it all started. And this is because for anger to become revenge is not a process that occurs within a single lifetime.

The seed of anger must first grow into a tree, i.e., it must get bigger, and when it starts bearing fruits, all the default patterns convert into deeds that cause harm to others. And so, due to unresolved anger, Peter can become so dangerous to those around him that he can be isolated or ostracised. At that stage of his evolutionary journey, this becomes his prarabdha karma—the karma Peter will have to deal with. And it will feel punishing, ultimately leading to a deeper realisation.

Thus, the event between Sam and Peter, where Peter, as a thief, robs Sam, is not where their karma ends. It only settles the transactional exchange (visible karma) between them, as determined by the karmic law. What remains pending is something much bigger than the event itself—the task of dissolving the seed of karma which is the tendency of greed and anger. And it is their invisible karma that exposes them to the dangers of accumulating more visible karma (give and take) with other souls.

Getting rid of invisible karma is the ultimate mandate of all karmic experiences. And to achieve this, one must first see karma as the seed, not just the fruit. The seed, or the tendency, when ignored for too long and acted upon too frequently, leads to misdeeds and increases one's negative karmic balance. In this way, it keeps a soul trapped in the cycle of cause and effect.

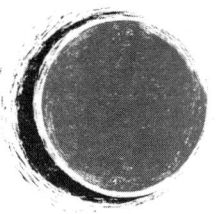

7

A Deeper Understanding
of Tendencies

As we try to understand how karma is created, it is important to first thoroughly investigate the root cause of karma—our tendencies. These tendencies are the seeds from which all forms of energy exchange emerge, making it essential to examine them closely. However, before diving into the nature of these tendencies, we must first explore their quality.

The ancient yogic scriptures, as well as other ancient and medieval Indian texts, refer to this quality as *gunas*. Guna means quality or attribute, and there are three types of gunas: *satva, rajas,* and *tamas.* Let's explore each of these in detail.

1. **Satva**

   Satva qualities emerge from one's spiritual nature. They help a soul retain the purity of character, remain uncorrupted, and stay aligned with their higher self.

Souls with dominant satva tendencies are closer to their original spiritual nature. Even though they are in the world, they do not derive their sense of self from it. They are less identified with worldly labels and concepts because they remain connected to their spiritual truth. This means these souls do not need to seek these qualities externally, as they are inherently empowered. Hence, they act as observers of worldly matters, yet they do not escape the world but fully participate in their interactions. These interactions are guided by the purity and power of their high-vibration character. And so, when satva-driven souls engage with the world, they operate through tendencies of peace, power, wisdom, and happiness, making their interactions more meaningful and impactful.

Tendencies with the quality of satva lead to intentions, thoughts, and actions that are selfless and guided by wisdom, truth, and righteousness. Such tendencies result in pure and meritorious deeds that generate positive energy, foster spiritual growth, and enable freedom from karma. They preserve soul power because they are aligned with the soul's original (spiritual) nature. Moreover, they contribute to the greater good of the collective consciousness.

2. **Rajas**

Rajas qualities are driven by desires and selfish interests. A stronger presence of rajas indicates a shift away from one's original nature of peace, purity, happiness, and power, leading to a dependency on external life to fulfil these needs. As a result, dominant rajas tendencies keep one immersed in worldly affairs, focused on personal gratification, and lacking inner strength. This dependency causes one to derive their sense of self from worldly things. Rajas qualities lower one's vibrational frequency compared to satva, resulting in ambition, anxiety, competitiveness, and desperation—all of which are rajas tendencies.

Tendencies with the quality of rajas lead to intentions, thoughts, and actions that are primarily self-centred, driven by personal interest and material gains. While they fulfil a soul's worldly desires, they contribute little to the greater good. Deeds influenced by rajas tendencies often result in low-intensity negative karma, as a soul under their influence loses some inner power and does little to empower consciousness. The greater danger of rajas tendencies lies in their potential to nurture the ego, which ultimately thrives in tamas. Therefore, a soul dominated by rajas qualities is susceptible to crossing over to the wrong side.

3. Tamas

Tamas qualities are driven by illusion and complete ignorance. They signify a soul that is disconnected from its spiritual nature and is more identified with the ego. The ego, as one's conditioned self, is accumulated over lifetimes through interactions with the material world. And the dominance of the ego destroys a soul's original capacity and powers, leading to deep identification with worldly concepts, labels, belief systems, opinions, people, society, possessions, and more. When driven by ego, a soul operates through tendencies of fear, anger, greed, lust, vanity, and attachment. These tendencies disempower the soul as they are negative and rooted in falsehood, opposing the soul's true nature. Tamas tendencies create a low-vibration character which contribute negatively to the world.

Tamas qualities lead to intentions, thoughts, and actions that are harmful and driven by ego and ignorance. These tendencies cause a soul to lose significant inner power and purity, creating disharmony and imbalance both within the soul and in its external environment. The deeds arising from such tendencies are often destructive in nature. They produce high-intensity negative energy, depleting power from the collective consciousness by causing harm and suffering to the self and others. This negative energy eventually returns as karmic debts.

Thus, if our tendencies are the seeds of karma (both good and bad), it is their gunas that determine the quality of these seeds. And one can refer to tendencies through their original quality. Additionally, satva, rajas, and tamas tendencies can be further classified into primary and secondary tendencies, with secondary tendencies emerging from the primary ones. When we observe a soul operating predominantly through secondary tendencies, it is essential to recognise that the root cause of their behaviour lies in the primary tendency. Moreover, a primary tendency can give rise to many secondary tendencies, but a secondary tendency results only in a certain type of behaviour and does not lead to the creation of tertiary tendencies. Therefore, it is the primary tendencies that define the conditioning, habits, and character of a soul's personality. These primary tendencies need to be addressed if they are negative and strengthened if they are positive.

Overall, when it comes to karma correction, one can summarise it as follows:

1. To correct high-intensity negative karma, one needs to assess and dissolve their primary tamas tendencies.

2. To correct low-intensity negative karma, one needs to assess and dissolve their primary rajas tendencies.

3. To strengthen punya or good karma, one needs to reinforce their primary satva tendencies.

While paying attention to the self, in order to understand the nature of one's karmic debts—particularly invisible karma—it is essential to identify the primary cause of karma, which is always the primary tendency. This is the seed that must be identified. And based on the gunas, our primary and secondary satva tendencies include:

1. **Primary Satva Tendency:** Peaceful

   Secondary Satva Tendencies: A peaceful person is accepting, flexible, balanced, calm, forgiving, harmonious, contented, grateful, blissful, productive, and wise. Wisdom stems from inner peace, as one cannot absorb or reflect wisdom without peace.

2. **Primary Satva Tendency:** Powerful

   Secondary Satva Tendencies: A powerful person is independent, mature, rational, humble, loyal, selfless, secure, courageous, righteous, fair, and gritty.

3. **Primary Satva Tendency:** Pure

   Secondary Satva Tendencies: A pure person is real, honest, self-aware, helpful, empathetic, simple, sincere, compassionate, trusting, kind, appreciative, creative, and perceptive.

4. **Primary Satva Tendency:** Happy

   Secondary Satva Tendencies: A happy person is encouraging, light, easy-going, generous, reliable, jovial, optimistic, vivacious, active, appreciative, and enthusiastic.

5. **Primary Satva Tendency:** Loving

    Secondary Satva Tendencies: A loving person is good, caring, understanding, giving, nurturing, affectionate, devoted, and warm.

Based on the gunas, our primary and secondary rajas tendencies include:

1. **Primary Rajas Tendency:** Ambitious

    Secondary Rajas Tendencies: An ambitious person can also be dynamic, worried, persuasive, dissatisfied, unreasonable, secretive, argumentative, sycophantic, ruthless, and self-doubting (as ambition often stems from a need to prove something about the self).

2. **Primary Rajas Tendency:** Selfish

    Secondary Rajas Tendencies: A selfish person can also be unfair, calculative, self-absorbed, unpredictable, stingy, and irrational.

3. **Primary Rajas Tendency:** Obsessive

    Secondary Rajas Tendencies: An obsessive person can also be restless, desperate, impatient, stubborn, edgy, nervous, anxious, and a workaholic.

4. **Primary Rajas Tendency:** Passionate

    Secondary Rajas Tendencies: A passionate person can also be emotional, intense, driven, opinionated, and pushy.

And finally, based on the gunas, our primary and secondary tamas tendencies include:

1. **Primary Tamas Tendency:** Angry

   Secondary Tamas Tendencies: An angry person can also be sad, pessimistic, bitter, aggressive, and suspicious. In certain cases, they may also exhibit bullying behaviour.

2. **Primary Tamas Tendency:** Greedy

   Secondary Tamas Tendencies: A greedy person can also be cunning, unethical, discontented, dishonest, manipulative, and devious.

3. **Primary Tamas Tendency:** Attached

   Secondary Tamas Tendencies: Attachment can make one controlling, possessive, dominating, jealous, and prone to low self-esteem.

4. **Primary Tamas Tendency:** Fearful

   Secondary Tamas Tendencies: Fear can make one revengeful, resentful, critical, judgemental, insecure, lazy, and hostile.

5. **Primary Tamas Tendency:** Vain

   Secondary Tamas Tendencies: Vanity can also make one pompous, arrogant, extravagant, conceited, and narcissistic.

6. **Primary Tamas Tendency:** Ignorant

   Secondary Tamas Tendencies: An ignorant person can also be careless, disorganised, aimless, fickle, moody, insensitive, dull, chaotic, deluded, and destructive.

To sum up, tendencies are the root cause of all karmic complexities because one interacts with the world through their tendencies. As the tendency, so is the interaction and its subsequent consequences.

As discussed in previous chapters, tendencies used repeatedly create conditioning. When one operates through this conditioning, habits are formed, and habits that persist ultimately shape character. A soul responds to the world of forms through its character. Therefore, as the character, so is the quality of one's intentions, thoughts, feelings, actions, interactions, and eventual deeds.

Moreover, deeds are the outcome of one's interactions and have good, bad, or neutral consequences. It is the energy of these consequences that returns to us as karma. Thus, karma vibrates at the frequency of one's character. The only way to break the wheel of karma is by transforming one's character and aligning with one's higher nature, which is built on satva guna tendencies.

Section II
Karma: Method and Manifestation

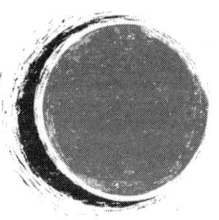

8

Types of Karma

*'Each man has a mission in life, which is the result
of all his infinite past karma.'*
—**Swami Vivekananda**

There are times when, despite our best efforts, we are unable to change the equation with certain people, and the relationship remains complicated. There are situations that continue to trouble us, no matter how patiently and efficiently we deal with them. Then there are moments when life feels unfair, and we suffer for no apparent fault of our own. At times, we see shrewd, cunning, and unscrupulous people living comfortable and prosperous lives, while those who are honest, kind, and simple struggle financially. This apparent unfairness leads us to question justice and doubt if it even exists. Some may even feel that staying on the right path is pointless and futile.

This is where understanding the types of karma becomes essential, as it brings clarity to the nature of events, relationship dynamics, and what is within our control versus what is not. While each of us must encounter different types of karma in life, understanding them helps us respond better to the circumstances, situations, and events that are integral to the karmic experience. This understanding helps us maintain equanimity and faith, especially in the face of extreme hardships and challenges, enabling us to navigate life with greater resilience and inner peace.

It also helps us see how karma restores justice and balance, often manifesting through life's environment, experiences, situations, circumstances, and events that carry valuable lessons and opportunities for the growth of character. However, before we explore the types of karma, we need to simplify the concept. For this, we use a metaphor.

Imagine you own an orchard filled with trees that bear different fruits in different seasons. In this orchard, new trees occasionally sprout and bear fruit, while old ones wither, are uprooted, or stop bearing fruit over time. Not all trees bear fruit simultaneously—different trees yield fruit in different seasons, and not all fruits ripen at the same time. But as and when they do, they are served to you.

The entire orchard represents your total accumulated karma across different lifetimes, symbolised by various trees and their seasonal fruit. When a particular tree bears fruit in a given season, you must consume some of it.

The seeds are the tendencies from which your karma trees grow. Each tree in the orchard holds the energy of the consequences of your deeds. This energy, like the tree itself, matures naturally and eventually bears fruit. The fruits you taste represent the karma you experience in a specific season or lifetime, and the seeds of these fruits were sown in prior lifetimes.

Furthermore, in each lifetime, since your tendencies remain active due to your interactions with the world, these interactions generate new deeds with new consequences. This means new energy either nourishes existing trees or helps new ones grow. Each new tree that emerges in this orchard symbolises new karma added to the total, while trees that wither or stop bearing fruit signify karma that has ended. Trees that continue to flower and bear fruit represent karma yet to be settled.

Thus, this metaphorical orchard is your subconscious, storing karmic recordings from all lifetimes. A soul continues to take rebirth until it ceases to add new recordings and erases all old ones, both of which constitute pending karma. In the context of the orchard, these recordings are represented by the trees.

Before we elaborate on the four types of karma, it is important to mention that the doctrine of karma finds its earliest reference in the ancient Hindu scriptures, the Vedas, among the world's oldest texts. The doctrine further evolved in the late Vedic texts called the Upanishads (a subsection of the Vedas), where it became associated with the principles of the afterlife and reincarnation, forming a comprehensive system for exploring and implementing wisdom with the aim of spiritual growth and enlightenment. It is from the Vedas and Upanishads that we derive the understanding of the four types of karma: *sanchita,* prarabdha, *kriyamana,* and *agami.* Let's explore them in detail.

1. **Sanchita**

   Sanchita karma is our total balance of karma, encompassing the energy of the consequences of all our past and present life deeds, which are to manifest as life experiences across different lifetimes. Sanchita comes from the Sanskrit word *sañcita,* meaning 'collected' or 'accumulated'. Thus, sanchita karma refers to the karma accumulated as the positive and negative consequences of our deeds in this life and all previous lives. These consequences bear fruit over different spans of time and across various births.

Some of these karmic consequences may be unfolding in the present, while others will manifest in future lives, depending on the maturity of the karma—much like the ripening of fruit, which follows its own natural course. Therefore, it is important to understand that sanchita karma, being the total burden of one's karma, cannot be experienced all at once. The fruits are served only when they mature and ripen.

2. Prarabdha

Prarabdha is the ripe fruit that must be served. It is that part of sanchita karma—our accumulated past-life karmas—that must be dealt with in the present. Prarabdha is the cause of our birth, and it challenges us mentally and emotionally because it serves a specific purpose: to help us clear our debts with the world around us. Therefore, from our sanchita karma, the negative karmas we are experiencing in this life constitute prarabdha. And the only way to end prarabdha karma is by experiencing it.

Our prarabdha karma is the pending karma from past births that we are meant to lessen or resolve in this lifetime. Since it is unavoidable, one must reap the effects of past-life karma. The results of these karmic effects unfold as intended—much like the taste of a fruit (bitter, sweet, sour, or bland), which depends on the seed sown in the past.

One could also say that prarabdha is the aspect of fate that must be endured. The experiences linked to it, in the form of situations, relationships, circumstances, and events, often bring unexpected difficulties for reasons beyond our understanding. While the experience of prarabdha is beyond our control, how we respond to it is within our control.

In Sanskrit, prarabdha means 'begun', 'commenced', or 'undertaken'. Thus, prarabdha karma represents the journey already underway for a soul as a result of past-life deeds and their respective consequences. Since this journey has already begun, its outcomes cannot be altered.

The truth about prarabdha is that it is irreversible, and it can be severe. In each lifetime, prarabdha karma determines our most significant experiences, influencing our situations, circumstances, events, relationships, and environment. The fruits of prarabdha, when experienced, can profoundly impact our inner state. Yet, in any negative scenario, acceptance and making peace with the situation can help one navigate this karma. However, this does not mean one should stop making efforts or give up. Rather, it means that whatever must be done to face or overcome challenges should be undertaken with unconditional acceptance of the situation and not with a desire for it to be different. Desires create anxiety, expectations, and negativity, which only further entangle karma. Accepting the pain, loss, or suffering that arises while dealing with this karma helps mitigate it, ultimately leading to freedom from it. The only way to find reprieve from prarabdha karma is by accepting the trials and tribulations that accompany it without giving up.

3. Kriyamana

If prarabdha is what we are to experience as the fruits of past karma, kriyamana is how we experience those fruits. How we respond to our present prarabdha is a choice we make using free will. Additionally, how we deal with prarabdha—and with life itself—creates new deeds with new consequences, which form our kriyamana karma. This karma gets added to our total balance of sanchita karma.

In Sanskrit, the word kriyamana means 'that which is being performed'. So, kriyamana karma includes what we are doing in the present moment. It is the karma being created by our current deeds and dominant tendencies, the fruits of which may be experienced now or in the future.

Thus, kriyamana karma is the energy we generate in the present. It influences our inner state and tendencies in ways that remain within our control, as we can exercise free will here. This free will is our power to respond to life experiences and prarabdha in a manner that supports our state of consciousness and prevents the further accumulation of karmic debts in our total balance of sanchita karma.

4. **Agami**

Kriyamana karma, in the form of our thoughts and intentions in the present life—those that could not translate into action or did not manifest as experiences but remained in the subconscious memory—also bears fruit in the future. This is agami karma.

Agami comes from the Sanskrit word *āgama,* which means 'coming near' or 'approaching'. Thus, agami karma is the fourth type of karma, which is to be experienced in future lives. It can also manifest as the realisation of desires that remained unfulfilled in the past.

Beyond these four types of karma, Vedic astrology further divides prarabdha karma into the following three categories

1. **Dridha Karma (Fixed)**

Dridha karma refers to high-intensity, fixed karma, whose results cannot be changed; they must be faced as they are. They cannot be altered due to the nature of past deeds, which may have been harsh and intentional, often backed by a rigid negative tendency.

Let's understand dridha karma through certain aspects of life.

a) A person with whom you are connected through this karma will inevitably be a part of your life and experiences, the nature of which is fixed.

b) In terms of wealth, if you are destined to encounter financial loss, you will be defrauded.

c) In matters of health, you may be born with a lifelong deformity or into a family with a history of genetic diseases, inheriting the same again due to fixed karmas or consequences beyond one's control, leaving no margin for change.

This means that if one has harmed someone or caused unpardonable physical, mental, emotional, or financial damage in the past, they will inevitably face the results of such deeds in this life. These results cannot be changed in any way. The only way to deal with this karma is by experiencing it.

2. Adhridha Karma (Easily changeable)

In this case, the results of karma are not fixed; they are mild in nature and can be altered by cultivating positive attributes, letting go of ego, and performing good deeds such as charity or engaging in intense meditative practices.

The component of free will remains active in *adhridha* karma, allowing for the alteration of results. This is because one's past deeds do not carry the weight of intentional harm done to someone, nor are they as severe as in the case of dridha karma. The results of adhridha karma are convertible or even avoidable, provided the free will is used to refine tendencies, elevate character, and reflect a positive shift in consciousness.

In different aspects of life, if adhridha karma is at play:

a) One can alter the prospects of being in a relationship tied to this karma, or the dynamics of the relationship can be changed.

b) The impact of financial losses can be mitigated through responsible and alert actions.

c) In terms of health, diseases can be overcome or even avoided through proper care, discipline, and effort.

3. Dridha Adridha (Difficult but Possible to Change)

Dridha adridha relates to what is fixed and unfixed. Its results may not be entirely avoidable but can be partially altered by facing challenges with patience, acceptance, effort, and goodwill. Dridha adridha karma also involves the use of free will but under testing circumstances. It challenges one's inner personality, demanding a major shift in consciousness, which requires significant self-awareness and self-work.

Dridha adridha karma arises from past-life deeds that were harsh but unintentional, i.e., where harm was caused without deliberate intent. This karma manifests in ways such as:

a) In relationships, you may end up with the same person to whom you unintentionally caused harm. Given the nature of this karma, the relationship will be difficult. However, if you use free will to endure and invest patience, resilience, and acceptance—without giving up prematurely—the difficulties will eventually resolve. They dissolve once your inner personality grows through humility and loss of ego.

b) The same principle applies to wealth and health issues. One must endure certain hardships, but these challenges foster humility rather than feeding the ego. Succumbing to despair, anger, hatred, or the desire for immediate change only reinforces suffering. The results of this karma are altered through sincere intentions and righteous action, gradually transforming the karma from intense to neutral.

A crucial point to understand after analysing the different types of karma is that life is not a punishment or an endless cycle of resolving difficult karmic debts. It is also about experiencing the rewards of our good deeds and the fortune attached to them. These good deeds, in ancient Vedic terminology, are described as *purva punya*.

In Sanskrit, *pūrva* means ancient or old, and punya refers to pious activities, virtue, or merit. Purva punya includes the merits and rewards of past actions, which are also part of sanchita karma. Such merits mature into present and future rewards, creating balance in one's life.

While we take birth to mitigate prarabdha karma, we also return to strengthen our virtues, accumulate merit, and enjoy the fruits of past good deeds. There are lifetimes when our purva punya or good karma outweighs our prarabdha, and vice versa. Both purva punya and prarabdha are present in every lifetime—only their degrees vary.

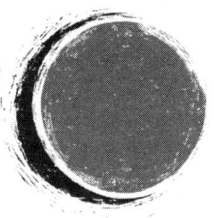

9

Prarabdha Karma:
Deeper Meaning and Purpose

Prarabdha karma is an opportunity to settle long-standing karmic debts. It also helps us understand the difference between fate and destiny, as prarabdha karma is an essential component of fate, while destiny is what we create in response to it. Fate results from past-life karmas, whereas destiny—the future—is scripted in the present through our kriyamana karmas. Moreover, only some aspects of fate are alterable, while destiny remains within our control. This depends on how well one responds to their prarabdha, which is crucial for dissolving even the toughest karmic debts. However, if one fails to do so, the experience of the same prarabdha karma may be prolonged and potentially carried over into future lifetimes, where it could become even more difficult to resolve.

The very purpose of life is freedom from karmic bondage, and prarabdha karma serves precisely this purpose. The heavier one's prarabdha in a given lifetime, the more karmic debts one is clearing. However, prarabdha karma is often dreaded because of its unpredictable and mysterious nature. The fear of our prarabdha can be even more discomforting when one does not understand oneself or the reasons behind their circumstances. Additionally, when one's character is clouded by egoic tendencies, prarabdha can feel even more perplexing and challenging. Yet, it is often our prarabdha that pushes us out of our comfort zones, demanding a positive shift in consciousness. It compels us to change and evolve, preventing stagnation or ignorance. This is one of the reasons it is feared—because change, though necessary, is often uncomfortable. Therefore, understanding the self through our given prarabdha is of greater significance than merely looking at prarabdha karma as a set of events or circumstances that are beyond our control.

Another crucial point is that a heavy prarabdha creates one of the finest environments for spiritual growth and maturity, as it offers greater opportunities for self-realisation and awakening. In contrast, a life with greater rewards from the past, or purva punya, does make self-realisation possible, but it carries the risk of straying from one's true purpose. This is because such a life may lack the challenges and suffering necessary to create a deeper sense of reality and truth. Furthermore, with each lifetime, our prarabdha shapes the circumstances and events essential for the growth of our consciousness. We suffer when we remain oblivious to this reality and view karma superficially, as something purely external.

To better understand our prarabdha, let us examine its two important facets.

1. It Takes Time to Return

The law of karma operates on pure math, not emotions. As a result, the consequences of our actions are often delayed, as it takes time for our sanchita karma to transform the energy of our deeds into the fruits of prarabdha. Therefore, time plays a crucial role in determining key aspects of prarabdha karma, which include:

- The magnitude of the consequence, or how much we must encounter or endure as prarabdha.
- Which aspects of our prarabdha are fixed and which are changeable.
- When and for how long we must experience this karma.

The shorter the time taken for a tree to convert the energy of our deeds into a ripe fruit, the smaller the fruit. This means that when the results of past deeds return as prarabdha karma, they are to be endured for a short time. However, the longer the energy of past deeds takes to return as karma, the bigger and heavier the fruit, implying that our karma could be intensely challenging depending on the circumstances and lessons it brings.

2. Its Effects Evolve

Some prarabdhas, as experiences, can be far more intense and painstakingly long to endure compared to others, which may be relatively easier and milder. However, what returns to us as the consequences of our deeds has a far greater effect or influence on us. In other words, the results of our deeds carry more weight than the original deed itself. This can again be metaphorically understood in terms of financial gains or losses.

For example, sound financial investments often yield returns with interest, whether in stocks, real estate, or jewellery, as they tend to appreciate over time. Similarly, the positive outcomes of our good deeds in any area of life return to us with added benefits, much like the appreciation of an investment. Therefore, karma retains the quality of the deed, ensuring that the good we invest in life brings back even greater good.

In the case of negative deeds or prarabdha karma, the consequences are comparable to a debt that must eventually be repaid, often with a penalty or interest. Just as failing to repay a loan can result in financial repercussions or even imprisonment, unaddressed wrongs in life carry their own form of punishment. Hence, when we face the consequences of our negative deeds, prarabdha karma has its own system of justice. It imposes a heavier penalty with a greater possibility of suffering.

In both instances, karma reflects the nature of the deed, ensuring that the quality of our actions determines the intensity of the consequences. So, what really is the ultimate purpose of prarabdha karma and how is this purpose served? Before we seek to understand this, we must recognise that everything happening under the law of karma serves a purpose greater than we may realise. And this purpose is the evolution of our state of consciousness through the purification of our tendencies.

Since a tendency is the seed of karma, it is responsible for the right and wrong in life, as whatever we do is influenced by a particular tendency, which eventually builds karmic debts or rewards. Until we discontinue using a negative tendency, we do not end the negative karma connected to it because deeds corresponding to this tendency keep manifesting in various scenarios.

For example, if person A harms person B out of anger, karma will return to punish A. However, person A can remain in karmic bondage due to their anger. Until there is realisation and correction of the tendency, person A will continue expressing anger in varying degrees, leading to similar deeds of different magnitudes involving different people. This, in turn, creates new consequences that evolve into progressively tougher prarabdhas over multiple lifetimes. The prarabdha becomes more challenging because a negative tendency, when reinforced over time, grows stronger and more self-destructive. It makes one's deeds more complicated and intense, resulting in tougher prarabdhas. However, an important point to clarify is that prarabdha is always earned; it is not created by some hidden force. It arises from the interplay of our tendencies and responses to life. So, for person A to break free, they must awaken and transition from anger to peace to end the continuity of karma.

The turning point in their journey would be their prarabdha with dridha karma—the karma that is fixed or unalterable and brings the most intense consequences. Enduring this prarabdha could mean suffering, and suffering is the greatest agent of change. While suffering eventually becomes unnecessary, its purpose is to trigger a deep realisation of what is truly wrong. This, in turn, leads to the purification of one's tendencies. Suffering cultivates humility, and humility helps us understand the truth. Truth, in turn, destroys ignorance or ego. And exposing the ego is the ultimate purpose of all karmic suffering.

Once their anger dissolves, person A's consciousness evolves, and their karmic bondage resulting from anger is broken. Thus, the purpose of any prarabdha is not punishment but the dissolution of a negative tendency.

Tendencies evolve over time through experiences. A positive tendency calls for reinforcement, while a negative tendency necessitates refinement of character. At times, strengthening a positive tendency requires a challenging environment. For example, someone with courage may be placed in circumstances that demand frequent acts of bravery, reinforcing their courage. Their prarabdha may assign them a role in the military, police, firefighting, or sports—fields that constantly require courage.

This illustrates that our experience of karma requires us either to extensively use a tendency (if positive) or to recognise and dissolve its self-destructive patterns (if negative). Ultimately, all negativity must be burned away in the fire of self-realisation.

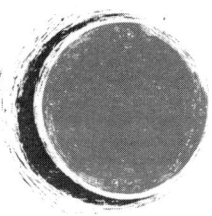

10

Subtle Workings of Karma

It is very interesting to explore how karma weaves its way into our lives, and how our karmic debts and balances can be understood against the backdrop of life's circumstances and situations. There is also a great deal of subtlety and peculiarity in the workings of karma, along with deeper revelations for the discerning mind. So, let's explore how karma works out the give-and-take through prarabdha.

We already know that karma takes time to return, i.e., the energy of our deeds, in the form of experiences (both rewarding and challenging), follows its own timeline. While we often view karma as a straightforward consequence of our actions, its workings are far more intricate. For example, in the case of a karmic settlement with another person, one might assume that meeting the same person again, in another form or identity in another life, is inevitable. However, this is not always the case. Re-encountering the same soul occurs only when both individuals have created significant karmic deeds that bind them to each other.

For instance, if you treat someone unfairly and cause them harm, leading to their suffering, this deed will carry certain consequences. If the other person responds with actions that perpetuate suffering, and both parties hold onto grudges, a karmic bond is formed. And when your respective prarabdhas ripen, you meet each other again in a different form, carrying unresolved energy from past conflicts.

In this new encounter:

- You will have to face the consequences of your past deeds.
- Resolve the previous conflict.
- Dissolve the tendencies that caused the conflict.

The goal of this encounter is:

- To break the cycle of negativity.
- Achieve harmony by resolving the differences.
- Foster growth.

However, this process becomes more difficult as it involves addressing not only the original conflict but also the consequences of your past actions and the tendencies that created them. And unless at least one person's actions and tendencies become more positive, the relationship between the two of you will not improve. However, a shift towards positivity elevates the frequency of the more positive individual beyond that of the karmic account, enabling them to exit the cycle and bring closure to their own pending karma in this exchange. If both individuals change for the better and accept their circumstances with dignity and peace, their karma ends. Furthermore, in another scenario, if their karmic account shows that only one of the two has created deeds of significant consequence in their prior exchange, then only that individual will have to face the results of their actions as prarabdha karma. The other person, who was merely at the receiving end of such deeds, can still exit the account if they owe no payback.

Let us understand this with an example.

Sam falsely accuses Peter of theft with the intention of maligning Peter's reputation. Peter feels humiliated and hurt but is unable to prove his innocence. They leave their present forms, and a karmic debt is credited to Sam's karmic balance sheet (sanchita karmas). Yet, Peter does not owe anything to Sam because he did not retaliate in ways that harmed Sam in any manner.

Now, Sam does not necessarily have to face the consequences of his deeds through Peter alone. When his prarabdha karma ripens, the same experience will be returned to him by someone else. This is because the workings of karma are designed to return the energy or results of one's deeds. These results can sometimes come from any source, particularly through those who resonate at the same frequency as the offender. In such cases, the experiencer (Peter) in the past encounter can be spared another interaction with the offender (Sam). The two souls need not remain entangled, especially when the experiencer owes nothing to the offender, as in this case.

Another scenario is when one of the two souls involved in the karmic exchange progresses in consciousness and moves to a higher frequency during the same lifetime in which the exchange took place. As a result, that particular soul, in its future lives, returns to the frequencies of their tendencies and fate rather than to the frequencies of the souls it was connected to through karma. This is why, when a soul progresses spiritually and grows in consciousness, it no longer aligns with people connected to it through a past energy exchange.

This can be further explored through another example.

Sam and Tara are married, but their relationship is strained due to anger issues, which make them incompatible. Sam expresses his anger through physical abuse toward Tara, while Tara, though she reacts to his behaviour, does not retaliate or harm him in any way. Instead, she internalises her emotions, creating emotional suffering for herself. While Sam's anger is outwardly directed and harms others, Tara's anger is repressed. It manifests as self-inflicted emotional pain in response to Sam's actions. Their incompatibility is further exacerbated by Tara's silent anger, which carries an energy that inadvertently fuels Sam's anger, creating a cycle of conflict.

After several years in the relationship, Tara decides to leave Sam. They separate, but their anger remains unresolved. As we have understood through the law of cause and effect in karma, if the energy of anger is not transformed, it will undoubtedly return as a key mandate of one's future prarabdha. And since Sam's actions involved physical abuse, his deeds carry severe consequences.

After walking out of her marriage, if Tara works on her anger and replaces it with peace, she will successfully raise her frequency. If she develops a more compassionate understanding of the situation that unfolded in her marriage and forgives Sam, holding no anger against him in her feelings or emotional memory, she will achieve tremendous growth in consciousness. Her silent forgiveness would also amount to some form of realisation for Sam, as forgiveness carries healing energy that one extends to their offender. By forgiving Sam and fostering the right feelings for him, Tara would completely let go of their ugly past. In doing so, she would achieve freedom from this soul connection. This is why forgiveness is an extremely important aspect of consciousness evolution and spiritual growth. Moreover, as Tara's frequency rises above the frequency of their karmic exchange, she would no longer be the one to deliver the consequences of Sam's deeds. Instead, someone at the same frequency as Sam's unresolved karma will align with him, allowing his karma to work through that source.

As for Sam, even if he feels repentant about his deeds, he will still need to experience their consequences. One might argue that if Sam feels repentant, shouldn't he be spared the consequences of his deeds? The answer is no. According to how karma works, the energy once created cannot be destroyed; it can only be transformed. Transformation occurs through graceful acceptance and the correct handling of the consequences of one's deeds by adopting the right tendencies. Thus, Sam cannot escape the consequences of his deeds. Until he experiences the prarabdha connected to his actions and transforms the negative energy attached to the results, he cannot fully resolve the pending karma. Any such transformation depends on how peacefully he handles these consequences, thereby altering the energy of his deeds and strengthening his character. However, with repentance in his psyche, it would be easier for Sam to face the consequences without further complicating his karma. Repentance carries the energy of realisation, which signifies a shift to a higher frequency. Consequently, the impact of his deeds may not affect him as severely as it would have if he had remained in his earlier state of ignorance. His karma would end only by experiencing the consequences and adopting the right attitude toward the inevitable suffering.

So, these examples reveal that the give-and-take between two souls does not necessarily keep them entangled for lifetimes. Further, since the subtle workings of karma are oriented toward strengthening one's satva nature (one's higher self), a soul with a dominant tendency toward peace might encounter a prarabdha with an environment that challenges their peace. For instance, consider the case of a family where the parents are in conflict, and the child grows up in an environment of discord. While different children respond differently to the same environment, a child with a dominant tendency toward peace is less likely to be affected by the negativity around them. By remaining an observer of what is—without judgement, expectation, or resistance—they could eliminate the possibility of trauma and further strengthen their peace. However, maintaining such an attitude is a matter of free will. Without exercising free will, tendencies do not evolve or dissolve.

To sum it up, karma essentially works on four mandates:

1. Settlement of past unfinished accounts and debts.
2. Closure of debts through the transformation of tendencies.
3. Freedom from undesirable tendencies.
4. Strengthening of empowering tendencies.

Additionally, prarabdha karma is worked out to achieve these mandates. It is the soul's own undertaking, which remains in the subconscious and cannot be fully comprehended by the brain alone. And prarabdha is based on three factors:

1. **Ripened Fruits:** The energy of past deeds that has now matured and must return to us as a karmic settlement. Its experience balances the equation of debt.

2. **Physical Environment:** The circumstances, situations, people, and events we need to encounter because of our past deeds.

3. **Experiences:** The influence of our outer reality on our inner state and the margin of free will that can be exercised.

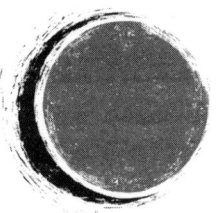

11

Sanchita Karma and Soul Recordings

*'Sanchita is all the accumulated karmas of the past.
Part of it is seen in the character of man, in his
tendencies and aptitudes, capacities, inclinations,
and desires.'*

—Swami Sivananda

Our inner personality is revealed through our behaviour
and our response to individual prarabdha, which includes
life situations, events, circumstances, and experiences.
Together, our inner personality and behaviour reveal
aspects of our sanchita karma. As discussed, sanchita is
our total balance of karma—both positive and negative—
recorded on the soul. This recording remains in the
subconscious and superconscious states of the mind.
The subconscious carries more recent recordings, while
the superconscious holds all possible recordings across
all births. These recordings exist as energy, and while we
are dealing with prarabdha karma, our sanchita karma
continues to influence us through this energy.

People with a low burden of sanchita are internally light because the nature of their soul recordings is light, preventing them from feeling heavy, bitter, or fearful of their prarabdha. A low burden of sanchita indicates a lower balance of pending negative karmas that could potentially convert into future prarabdhas. When this balance is low, the soul subconsciously feels lighter. Such souls treat their good fortune with care and responsibility, and you will rarely find them complaining about life. They are able to handle difficulties, even those that are part of a tough prarabdha.

The key takeaway is that the way one responds to their given prarabdha, as well as their good fortune (the rewards of past merits), reveals a great deal about their soul and its journey across lifetimes. The heavier one's burden of sanchita karma—accumulated negative karmas that are due to convert into prarabdha—the harder it is for a soul to respond wisely to life. Even when blessed with favourable circumstances, a person with heavy sanchita often struggles to handle matters wisely or comfortably.

For example, one may attain a position of power as a reward for good deeds from a past life. However, if their soul remains burdened with complex recordings or pending karmic debts, they may misuse this power, acting out of ego rather than wisdom. This strengthens their ego, leading to more fear and less clarity. Since karma can be described as an imprint or record etched onto the soul, its weight continues to influence the soul.

Just as someone under heavy financial debt remains under pressure, so too does a soul burdened with heavy sanchita karma. This unease arises from the soul's subtle states—the subconscious and superconscious. While the subconscious is often active in dreams or moments of inner stillness, the superconscious, which holds the most exhaustive recordings, remains inaccessible.

A person's active memory, connected to the brain, cannot access this recording because it contains vast amounts of data spanning several lifetimes. However, the superconscious functions like an archive, storing the complete record of a soul's deeds and tendencies across numerous forms. A few enlightened beings with highly developed spiritual and psychic abilities, in a state of superconsciousness—meaning heightened awareness—can fleetingly access small portions of this data, particularly in states of intense sadhana or meditation. Their insights may appear as flashes, providing clues to past lives and their associated energy or states of consciousness. For souls not engaged in intense spiritual sadhana, portions of this data may sometimes be revealed during past life regression. Science, too, has explored this area extensively, successfully helping individuals heal from traumas, physical pain, psychological blocks, relationship issues, and fears or phobias that were identified during such sessions as carryovers from past lives.

However, accessing this data in totality is both impossible and unhealthy, as it is vast, heavy, and exhausting. Moreover, it exists as a soul recording—

not in the form of facts and figures, but as energy. This energy influences an individual's responses to life, as it is experienced primarily through feelings rather than direct interpretation. When the recording is heavy, the associated feelings can be unsettling, leading to confusion in the mind. Depending on how one feels under this influence, one responds to life and its various aspects. Thus, even when their environment and circumstances appear comfortable, some people—whose soul recordings are heavy—respond to life in ways that seem contradictory. Conversely, there are those who, despite facing adversity, scarcity, or unfavourable circumstances, carry on with resilience and spirit.

Additionally, the ability to exercise free will is influenced by the energy of one's soul recordings. When the recording is heavy, using free will becomes difficult because the mind is perpetually noisy, drowning out the voice of intuition. Such individuals may be more prone to giving up rather than persevering through the challenges of their prarabdha.

An important aspect of resolving karma and leading a good life is cultivating awareness of one's soul recordings, as their energy is the energy of one's consciousness. And since consciousness drives behaviour and responses, it ultimately shapes the course of one's life.

Furthermore, one's behaviour provides the clearest insight into the state of their consciousness and the nature of their soul recordings. Typically, souls with a lighter recording or a low burden of sanchita karma remain stable even in the face of a difficult prarabdha. They exhibit the following characteristics:

a) They maintain optimism, gratitude, and a sense of inner calm.

b) Their inner environment is quiet and luminous.

c) Their mind is unburdened, uncluttered, and free from noise.

d) They have dominant satva tendencies.

e) They possess low ego and high intuition.

Such individuals are more likely to handle their prarabdha correctly. Even if it is heavy due to the late maturity of deeds performed several lifetimes ago, it does not dampen their spirits.

Though souls with a heavier burden of sanchita karma and complex soul recordings are likely to remain unstable, even if they have an easy prarabdha and good fortune. What is more:

a) Their inner environment is complicated, as they are easily influenced by the negative promptings of stored energy through feelings.

b) Their mind is noisy due to a heavy subconscious, which reduces their ability to discern with clarity.

c) They are inclined toward negativity, fear, insecurity, exaggeration, attachment, pessimism, doubt, overthinking, overanalysis, complaining, comparison, and criticism.

d) They have dominant tamas and rajas tendencies.

e) They have a high ego, which blocks intuition and creates confusion.

Finally, there is a third category—people with a medium burden of sanchita karma, neither too high nor too low. They exhibit a combination of traits and behaviours from the other two categories. While they are on the road to recovery, they still fluctuate between peace and chaos.

To conclude, our sanchita karma does not go silent once prarabdha becomes active in a given lifetime. Sanchita continues to influence us. However, through higher self-awareness and consistent self-work, one can overcome its negative effects.

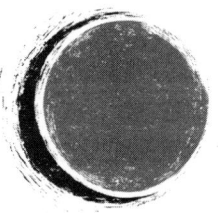

12

Understanding the Burden of Karma

*'No man is to be judged by the mere nature of his
duties, but all should be judged by the manner and
the spirit in which they perform them.'*
—Swami Vivekananda

We often perceive eminent positions such as heads of organisations (including spiritual or religious ones), heads of state, armies, companies, businesses, or even public figures as truly privileged. However, the truth is that such individuals carry far more karma to burn than an ordinary person. This is because the greater one's duty and responsibility towards others and the larger one's field of interaction, the heavier one's burden of karma.

So, when observing the lives of leaders, public figures, or heads of any establishment, one must also consider:

1. Their extensive interaction with the world of forms.

2. The significant amount of public dealings they must navigate.

3. Their responsibility to contribute to society.

4. The relentless scrutiny and pressure they endure.

5. The difficult decisions they make, and how often these impact a large number of people.

6. Their constant state of busyness.

7. The pressure to keep everyone happy, satisfied, or entertained (particularly in the case of entertainers).

8. The employment opportunities they must generate to help people earn their livelihood.

9. The personal time they must sacrifice.

It is vital to understand that a life of fame, affluence, and power is not a perk but a massive responsibility and duty, forming part of a substantial karmic payback. And so, even though the lives of powerful individuals may appear privileged, comfortable, or even glamorous, they must work much harder than the average person. This is because their soul has undertaken the task of clearing a significant portion of karmic debts. Their heavy burden of karma in the present life, along with their privileges, results from multiple debts and rewards of past karma maturing simultaneously. So, the fruit of their present prarabdha is heavy, but so is their purva punya, or past merits.

Therefore, when some souls enjoy higher status, power, fame, or wealth, their prarabdha is also an opportunity to settle more karma within a short time—meaning a much larger load of pending karma is to be worked out in one life. This shows that, from a karmic perspective, life revolves around two aspects:

1. Circumstances or environment which represent fate.
2. Mandate which is the purpose of life and what we are meant to create as destiny.

These aspects apply to everyone. The mandate involves character refinement and the settlement of pending karma, which is intertwined with life events, situations, and relationships—everything that forms part of our circumstances. Our future or destiny depends on fulfilling this mandate. The way we deal with it contributes new energy to our sanchita karma, which is bound to return as fate.

Therefore, even though people in prominent positions or with great wealth and affluence have favourable circumstances, their mandate is not just about enjoyment, pleasure, or indulgence. The fact that it requires hard work, expansion, growth, relevance to society, building lives, creating opportunities for others, and being selfless, kind, compassionate, and in service to those less fortunate shows that the mandate is much more. This is how they are meant to dissolve a significant burden of karma.

So, their prarabdha is heavy, yet it favours them in terms of circumstances because they also bring plenty of rewards from past merits or good karma. But what does this indicate about their sanchita karma or their soul recordings? Is it heavy or much lighter? The answer lies in how these seemingly privileged souls respond to their fortune or prarabdha. If they display signs of ego and fail to fulfil their responsibilities with humility, sincerity, fairness, and righteousness—amounting to *dharma*—it indicates that their burden of sanchita karma or their soul recordings is heavy. They may be born into or may have risen to lives of great abundance, power, fame, or prominence, but without humility, diligence, righteousness, compassion, honesty, generosity, and truth, their present life is wasted. The absence of such virtues indicates ego, and with ego, even though their life presents a grand opportunity to burn karma on a large scale, and even though it stems from the rewards of good deeds from past lives, it does not necessarily point to good sanchita karma or a low burden of the same.

Here, it is important to understand that the law of karma operates with absolute impartiality. It is devoid of emotions, mercy, forgiveness, or leniency in its calculations. There is no favouritism, no bias—only the truth. One reaps exactly what one has sown.

At times, we observe individuals who seem undeserving and operate out of extreme ego leading the most privileged lives. This often puzzles us. But this happens because good deeds from their past lives have matured collectively at the same time, converting into rewards within a single life. And so, the karmic math is in their favour.

Perhaps lifetimes ago, these souls donated wealth, protected others, or supported the masses in ways that benefited many. The fruits of those actions have now ripened, allowing them to enjoy these rewards. Thus, the ripened fruits of seeds sown many lifetimes ago now manifest as their present life's fate or fortune. Yet, like the temporary nature of life, these fruits too perish with time. So, while one may see someone enjoying the rewards of past merits, if they are not creating good deeds in the present or are not egoless, they are merely exhausting the good they have accumulated—showing that their privileged fortune is only a temporary boon.

Therefore, the next time you see seemingly undeserving individuals living their best lives or deserving ones enduring challenges, refrain from questioning or feeling enraged. Simply understand—it's all temporary. Temporary rewards and temporary punishments. And all a matter of fortune and prarabdha in a given life.

While prarabdha can be worked out and some of its results even avoided, one cannot escape its fixed component. And to successfully handle one's prarabdha, one must understand two key aspects:

1. Situational

The situational aspect relates to what we have and involves the opportunity to interact with a specific set of people, in a specific geography, under specific circumstances, and within a specific family and society. This is because of an energy exchange from the past, with pending debts or karma, involving the souls in those environments. For instance, in the case of public figures, organisational heads, or those in seats of power, there is always an element of give and take—and on a much larger scale. Without the support of the masses or the people who work for them, they cannot maintain their worldly status, enjoy the spotlight, or hold positions of authority and financial abundance. Thus, for powerful, influential, and famous individuals, the exchange of energy happens through significantly large numbers of interactions, and only through these can they bring closure to their pending karmic debts.

2. Behavioural

The behavioural aspect determines what we do with what we have. Either someone will take their heavy prarabdha as an opportunity to settle long-pending karmic debts, or they will become bitter and reject their mandate at the whims of their ego—only increasing their karmic bondage.

Also, when someone fails to fulfil the purpose of their individual prarabdha despite favourable circumstances, they may have to repeat the karmic cycle under tougher conditions. This happens because when life offers favourable circumstances despite heavy prarabdha—like in the case of powerful or affluent individuals—the margin for error is very small. If these favourable circumstances are not used to create good deeds and cultivate a high-vibration character, tougher lifetimes await these souls. They must return with the same mandate but under far more challenging conditions. Let us understand this through an example.

Peter is a successful and wealthy industrialist, but he is unkind to his employees. Their salaries are inadequate for their efforts, they are made to work long hours, and they are not paid on time. Meanwhile, Peter continues to flourish, expanding his wealth and business, while his employees remain unhappy. Peter's circumstances are a test of his character. Since he does not exhibit purity of character, he is only complicating his karmic accounts with his employees.

In his next lifetime, Peter will have to repeat these interactions—but under a different equation where his privileges, affluence, and power will cease to exist. Yet, he must repay his karmic debts because he acted unfairly in the previous exchange.

This example illustrates that with life's privileges come responsibilities. Only by handling these responsibilities with due diligence can one settle significant karmic debts. To falter in the behavioural aspect, especially when circumstances are supportive, is to waste a great opportunity for spiritual growth and the offsetting of heavy karma.

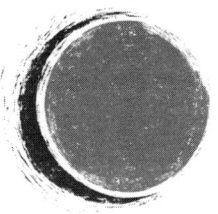

13

Why Do Some Good Souls Get a Challenging Prarabdha?

As discussed in earlier chapters, sanchita karma is not only the accumulation of the consequences of our deeds across various lifetimes but also the accumulation of tendencies shaped by satva, rajas, and tamas gunas. This means that we are distinct individuals with a unique fate, life path, and behaviour, carrying different burdens of sanchita karma.

Prarabdha karma, on the other hand, offers an opportunity to reduce the burden of sanchita karma—in essence, a chance to transform the energy of our negative karmas. However, there are times when it is difficult to assess whether a person's total burden of karma (sanchita) is high or low. The confusion arises when we see good people or those with dominant satva traits (high-vibration tendencies) encountering an extremely challenging life or prarabdha. Their situations, events, or circumstances appear to be in stark contrast to their character.

However, despite this, what appears to be suffering due to our limited perspective is actually an opportunity for accelerated spiritual growth. Without understanding this, one might mistakenly believe that life or the divine forces are unjustly punishing good souls. It is, therefore, crucial to view such scenarios with wisdom and recognise that a challenging prarabdha serves a greater purpose beyond what the human mind can easily grasp. Let's explore how.

1. Good Souls Get to Settle More Karma in Less Time

A challenging prarabdha may result from the late and sudden maturity of past negative karmas, often carrying a heavier penalty and requiring one to face multiple challenges at once. However, for good souls, this too is an opportunity—to clear more karmic debts in less time and accelerate spiritual growth. With a heavier prarabdha bringing major relief from karmic debts, what is perceived as hardship is, in fact, liberating. Not only does it create more room for learning and maturity, but it also helps the soul erase several unwanted recordings in just one lifetime— almost akin to settling a bank loan in one go rather than spreading it across several years and instalments. Additionally, good souls can handle a heavier burden because they have the capacity to do so. What may take other souls several lifetimes to settle can often be completed by these souls within a single or a few lifetimes. This is primarily because good souls have high-vibration energy, enabling them to endure greater challenges without breaking or succumbing to the pressures of life. And it is the purity and power of their character that makes settling karma easier— unlike those who, under the influence of ego, waste time resisting the settlement by spending a large part of their lives blaming, complaining, and questioning everything.

Some even resort to rituals and remedies to abort the course of karma, which only intensifies its results and tightens their karmic knots, making their burden even heavier. This happens because when negative life situations and tendencies are left unaddressed and unchanged, they add more negativity to one's existing karmic balance, leading to even more severe consequences. Thus, the soul's suffering intensifies until it awakens to the truth and takes the necessary steps for damage control.

However, good souls, who operate at a higher frequency, inherently understand what is empowering and what is depleting, and they choose to remain at a higher frequency, which enables them to discern and walk the path to freedom.

For example, in a journey undertaken on a dark night, some people, when they lose their way, become petrified and perplexed and remain stuck due to fear and confusion. Not knowing what to do next, they wait for someone to rescue them or for dawn to break. But since different people face the same situation differently, there are those who are fearless and think with clarity. They do not reject the situation or create more chaos. Instead, by using their intuitive sense, they find their way to their destination. Good souls are the latter kind. They are intuitively aligned with their destination and do not fear or avoid the challenges of life. Hence, they do not postpone karmic settlement.

2.   Good Souls Evolve by Continually Improving

Good souls, when their character is put to the test, are likely to emerge stronger. Take the example of the human body which derives its strength from its muscles. The more these muscles are used, the stronger the body becomes. But for this to happen, the body must remain active, pushing its boundaries and experiencing discomfort—something we all encounter when we exercise or engage in physical activity.

Similarly, the power of the soul lies in its positive tendencies. And the more these tendencies are exercised or used in challenging situations, the more powerful the soul becomes. This is why good souls find themselves in tough environments where they must push their boundaries and use their positive tendencies to the fullest. In this way, the extreme situations and events of their lives—their tough prarabdha—act as the alchemist that turns them into pure gold. With a difficult life, these souls get countless opportunities to apply their positivity in negative situations, which is by far the most effective way to deepen character. For only when one does not succumb to the pressures of negativity but instead uses their positive tendencies to remain steadfast, does positivity grow, and karma dissolves faster. This happens because one raises their frequency and rises above the negative energy field of prarabdha.

Thus, we can say that the karmic mandate for good souls is to master goodness. Because when positive tendencies are applied in negative circumstances, they deepen character. Moreover, it is the power of character that helps one settle most of the accumulated burden of karma and attain freedom. Consider some revered sages, mystics, and spiritual masters of the past who attained liberation from karmic bondage purely through the strength of their character. Some of them faced the most challenging prarabdha, having sacrificed all forms of materiality. Yet, despite their physical hardships, they did not react emotionally but simply observed life without judgement or inner noise. They did not surrender the power of their positive tendencies; rather, they harnessed them to create a life that was nothing short of miraculous. In their presence, people felt healed, comforted, and transformed—something that naturally occurs when low-frequency souls enter the energy field of high-frequency souls. This field, charged with purity and positivity, facilitates healing. And healing is nothing but realigning souls who are unable to access their higher state of being due to misalignment with their spiritual nature.

3. Good Souls Help Raise the Vibration of the Planet

The planet is inhabited by countless life forms, each possessing energy. This energy becomes either additive or destructive when the discretionary mind is attached to it. The discretionary mind, or intellect, when used in a certain way, creates energy with consequences that not only influence all other energy beings but also affect the overall energy and environment of the planet.

Among all living species, only humans have intellect and the ability to use the discretionary mind. This makes the intellect a powerful human faculty. While all other living beings focus on survival and coexistence, maintaining the order and balance of their environment, humans create deeds with both positive and negative consequences, depending on how they use their intellect. Positive actions benefit the environment, whereas negative ones cause turbulence and destruction.

The way humans use their intellect largely depends on their dominant tendencies. Positive tendencies lead to creation, while egoic tendencies cause destruction. This is why it is crucial to have people who use their intellect to create positive outcomes and foster a harmonious environment. However, the right use of intellect is only possible when souls operate at a higher frequency. This is why good souls are essential.

Here, it is vital to understand that when their prarabdha is challenging, good souls use positivity with greater resolve and intensity. As they apply their positive tendencies while facing adversity, they not only use their intellect in the best possible way but also generate energy that creates a positive environment for others. Their very behaviour emits energy that uplifts those at a lower frequency and serves as a catalyst for change. It inspires those struggling in their darkest moments, helping them discover ways to find their own light.

This is because positivity holds greater power than negativity, and the only antidote to negativity is positivity itself. In subtle ways, good souls—or high-frequency souls—counter negativity. Furthermore, it is not difficult to recognise them: people who smile even in their darkest times, who remain stable in challenging scenarios, who help others even when they themselves are in need, who do not waste time complaining, criticising, or blaming others for their hardships. People who do not engage in conflicts driven by ego, who do not allow their peace to shatter or their happiness to succumb to life's difficulties.

Thus, good souls, much like the rays of the sun, help build the immunity of all living beings on the planet and support lower-frequency souls in maintaining balance—something the latter struggle to achieve on their own due to the deficiencies of their character. This is why good souls must endure challenges; they burn to shine, illuminating the path for others and fulfilling a higher purpose.

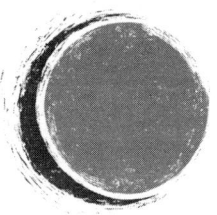

14

Kriyamana Karma:
The Power in Your Hands

A seed, once sown, takes time to become a plant, and a plant takes time to grow into a fruit-laden tree. The seed does not bear fruit immediately. Thus, we can say that nature runs its course—maturing, growing, and yielding results over time. Such is karma. The seeds we sowed many lifetimes ago are bearing fruits today, just as the seeds we plant now will shape our future. And though we are always fixated on the fruits in hand, what matters most is the seed we are sowing now. Put simply, while the past may have shaped our present, we have a say in our future. In fact, it is the only thing within our control. This is referred to as kriyamana karma—the karma we create in the present moment through our active tendencies and deeds.

Our energy exchange with other souls on this journey depends on our behaviour, thoughts, words, and actions, which shape our environment and life. Destiny, then, is the result of our present-day deeds and tendencies, which remain active while we also respond to the consequences of past actions. Thus, our human journey is a constant interplay of energy—between the unfolding consequences of past deeds, known as prarabdha karma, and the new consequences created by our present actions, known as kriyamana karma.

How we respond to prarabdha karma and to our complete experience of life constitutes kriyamana karma—the force that determines our future and sows the seeds of destiny. So, man does make his own destiny. However, destiny becomes complicated when we fail to act in the present moment or fail to direct our attention and energy where it is needed. Ultimately, as the law of karma dictates, we are always faced with the results of what we create.

The fact is that in this human journey, we are meant to progress using our prudence (intellect) and free will which are the two most important faculties of the soul. And it is our character that directs these faculties, driving us to create deeds that bear consequences and shape our destiny. Therefore, character plays a crucial role in both the creation and dissolution of karma. And while we may have the purest of intentions, unless we create the right deeds and shape our character, we cannot exit or escape karmic bondage. Further, at every step, the choices we make and the way we respond to life not only influence the quality of our sanchita karma—our soul's accumulated record—but also shape the fate we will encounter in future lives as future prarabdha. Therefore, if we wish to end karma or avoid creating further negative karma, we must place greater emphasis on our character, our choices, and our responses.

When we choose to respond wisely to challenging people and situations, we create good kriyamana karma, the results of which secure both our present and future. When we no longer generate negativity, we break the cycle of negative karma and change the course of destiny.

And when it comes to destiny, there are two parts to it. One is the turn of events, experiences, and energy exchanges shaped by the consequences of our good or bad deeds from past lives—this is fate, which includes prarabdha karma.

As for the second part, it is being written in the present moment based on the way we face the rewards or punishments of our past life deeds. Therefore, we can either choose to better ourselves in the present moment and, in doing so, strengthen our future, or we can choose to give up, get carried away, and fail to face our karma correctly, which complicates both the present and the future. Because, depending on our response to life and the wisdom (or lack of it) that we apply, we can either write a destiny of pain or a destiny of peace.

The important thing to remember is:

1. We have the power to choose our response to life.
2. We have the power to create our own destiny.

This has been an undeniable part of our journey since forever. And this power is the power of our kriyamana karma. Its significance is underscored by the fact that our karmic debts do not get resolved by thinking about the past or dwelling on what may have happened. Rather, our debts are only resolved by taking action in the present, i.e., by taking charge and performing deeds that bring more positivity to our life situation and to ourselves. Thus, to break the wheel of karma, we must value the present and invest ourselves completely in it. We need to empower our character and our deeds because that is what creates high-vibration kriyamana karma. The vibration separates us from past negativity and helps us rise above the consequences of past karma. It also positively influences the overall quality of our accumulated karmas and contributes to creating a good future.

Put simply, regardless of how tough life may be today, if we choose to operate out of wisdom, remain positive and calm, and send out the right energy to our future, we will surely manifest the life we want to live. Remember, the future is in our hands, and it lies in the choices we make today and in the tendencies we cultivate more actively.

Section III
Karma: Course of Action

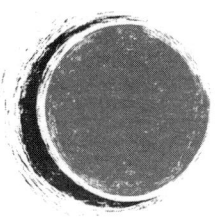

15

How to Handle
Difficult Prarabdha

Life is unpredictable because elements of our past exist in the present, and we are all riding the waves of prarabdha karma, moving from one shore to another. These waves are a small part of the vast ocean of sanchita karma, which consists of everything we have lived and created so far. But what happens when the ocean gets rough, and the waves become unmanageable? In other words, how does one move past a difficult prarabdha?

Given the nature of prarabdha, it is important to recognise that not all of life is challenging, and therefore, life itself cannot be labelled as difficult. Some aspects of life are governed by dridha karma (fixed karma), which remains unchanged despite our best efforts. However, there are also aspects where challenges can be easily overcome (adridha karma), allowing us to change our life situations for the better. Then there are some aspects that can be changed but would require extra effort and perseverance (dridha adridha karma). With this understanding, let's explore ways to successfully move past a challenging prarabdha.

1. Don't Paint the Entire Canvas Black

When you begin to view your life through the lens of fixed and difficult-to-alter karmas, you may easily succumb to pressure. You stop using your inner powers and start feeling like a victim of circumstances. This is unhealthy, as it creates a state of hopelessness that prevents you from dealing effectively with life, people, and various situations. It blocks you from using your free will to alter that component of prarabdha which can be easily changed. As a result, you begin operating at a lower frequency, feeling drained, and developing a negative outlook. The ego strengthens in the form of anger, low self-esteem, fear, insecurity, and unfulfilled desires. You want things to change, but you do nothing about it because now you see your whole life as one big problem. You become fixated on the difficulties, completely overlooking the aspects that are good. This further complicates your prarabdha, because your energy—through attention—goes only to the negative, thereby making the negative stronger.

The first step, therefore, is to stop painting the entire canvas of life black and cultivate the ability to identify and regularly acknowledge the positive aspects. Regardless of how small or insignificant they may seem, they deserve more of your attention. Doing this helps break the momentum of negativity and elevates your energy to a higher frequency, from which you can begin finding solutions to life's challenges. Remember, until your energy shifts to a higher frequency, your life does not change. However, when you move to a higher frequency—by changing your outlook to a more positive one—your vibe changes, and you begin to attract more solutions than problems.

2. Remind Yourself It's Only Temporary

Your prarabdha karma and fortune are as temporary as your human journey. So, regardless of how challenging or pleasurable they may be, there is no need to become too attached to them. Attachment means responding through the ego, which leads to unhealthy tendencies. Additionally, attachment causes you to become like your bundle of prarabdha, So, if it is challenging, you become negative and weighed down by the burden, denying the possibility of change. This keeps you stuck in a whirlpool of struggle, pain, and misery (a low-vibration energy field).

Similarly, in the case of good fortune, attachment can lead to a fear of loss or a desire to remain where you are. In both cases, you negate the temporary nature of life, resulting in excessive identification with the transient world of forms.

When you realise the temporary nature of life and everything connected to it, you can accept and experience it without attachment. This means remaining a detached observer of people and situations, without reacting through low-vibration tendencies or the ego, which only amplifies suffering or deepens illusions about one's prarabdha and fortune. Additionally, understanding that things are temporary doesn't mean passively waiting for a challenging prarabdha to pass. If you do, you are still attached to it, still at its negative frequency. The ideal approach is to observe without absorbing, i.e., retaining your inner peace and balance by not creating judgements or opinions about what is.

Judgements intensify our conflicts. When we judge someone or something, we reject them in our minds, creating more negativity in our own energy. This negativity transmits to the situation, further intensifying it, thereby generating more suffering and conflict.

3. Surrender and Accept What Is Fixed

In life, we are often oscillating between acceptance and resistance. This happens when we desperately want things to be how we think they should be, rather than accepting how they are. We fail to understand that some things in life simply cannot be the way we want them to be. This is where resistance fills us with questions, worries, expectations, analysis, anger, and doubt, complicating our experience of life and the karma attached to it.

Resistance creates stress, conflict, control, and bias towards what is. In essence, resistance is selfish. It represents our dislike, contempt, and rejection of what contradicts our expectations. Since all three carry negative energy, they change nothing outside of us. Not only does resistance extend the karmic experience, but it also prolongs the suffering created by the mind, which remains in opposition to the situation and its karmic experience.

Another thing to note here is that what we resist is likely to persist, thus extending our experience of karma. Since karma only exists in our circumstances, situations, or relationships, when we create resistance and suffering in response, we make it a part of our being. This keeps it alive in us and in our soul recordings, which can be easily avoided by allowing things to be as they are and shifting our focus to what can be changed for the better.

Acceptance, on the other hand, is when we stop trying to control challenging situations or people to mould them according to our wishes. We accept what is 'as-is' and put an end to the conflict between the self and the situation that is karmically linked to us, thereby preventing it from damaging our inner environment. This does not mean that if someone is causing us harm, we must continue to suffer silently. It means we do whatever is necessary for our own well-being without reacting to the situation because karma attains continuity through our reactions.

Overall, acceptance of the unalterable helps us avoid wasting time and energy fighting it or wishing it were different. This applies to a life situation, a relationship, or our circumstances. And if something or someone does not change according to our liking, despite our best efforts, we must recognise that it is fixed karma.

The fixed component of prarabdha is what tests us the most. It consumes our time and energy because, in the end, it must teach us acceptance, humility, and surrender. However, some people, out of ignorance, continue to fight it all their lives, only to be dragged down in the process. These individuals only increase the severity of their challenges because, through resistance, they neither settle what is pending nor overcome egoic tendencies, which further complicates their karma. Therefore, it is crucial to understand that what cannot be changed is present in our lives for a reason. It is there as part of our biggest karmic settlement.

4. Choose the Right Frequency and Response

When facing a challenging prarabdha, remind yourself that you have no control over the storm, but you surely have control over yourself. And when you remain calm, the storm shall pass. Why? Because you will rise above the storm, and it will no longer remain connected to your frequency.

The storm here implies karmic events, situations, and relationships that are challenging but can be altered, provided we experience them with composure and operate through high-frequency tendencies. When we succumb to the pressures of karma due to operating through low-frequency tendencies, we add unhealthy recordings to the subconscious. Any such recording increases the burden of karma or makes the prarabdha more rigid and complex.

For example, if you are stuck in a close relationship where the other person behaves contrary to your expectations and consistently does the opposite of what you want, then clearly, there is karma in the equation. If you remain at a low frequency and respond with anger, disputes, or a constant mental commentary criticising them, they are likely to intensify your annoyance and continue their behaviour. This happens because you are responding through the frequency of resistance. But when you remain at a higher frequency and maintain inner stability despite their nuisance, you can alter your experience of karma. This means that while the person remains the same (especially if you share fixed karma with them), you respond in ways that neither damage you nor negatively trigger them. Thus, the difficult karma reveals itself as it is meant to, but since you don't react negatively, the experience of that karma remains short-lived, i.e., you don't add more force or momentum to it. As a result, the person may either remove themselves from your life, or if they stay, you find effective ways to deal with them.

Another possible scenario where karma is easily alterable is when a person, influenced by your positive energy, undergoes a positive transformation. Even in cases where karma is alterable with effort, transformation can occur if you maintain inner silence. In all such situations, change is only possible when you do whatever is necessary externally while maintaining a higher frequency internally. This means no inner noise—no complaints, criticism, conflict, anger, or stress—just detached observation of what is.

This approach works even in worst-case scenarios (fixed karma), where two people must part ways due to differences. Their karma may result in separation, but despite the negativity of the situation, if there are no grudges, complaints, anger, or acrimony, one no longer remains in the energy field of that karma, and it ends. However, if negativity persists even after separation, the karma gets extended.

One must always remember that positive energy is far superior to negative energy, and negativity cannot last long in the presence of a strong positive force. Additionally, two negatives don't make a positive; instead, they intensify the negativity because their frequencies match. However, when one person chooses to remain at a higher frequency in the face of karmic challenges, no additional negativity is added to what is already negative. Instead, in a clash of frequencies, the negative weakens and becomes ineffective.

The main takeaway here is that although our conditioned mind likes to believe that karma has immense influence and power, the truth is that real power lies in the response of the experiencer. If the experiencer is powerful, karma loses all power. Even in situations where we may not have much choice, we can still choose our response (frequency) carefully. When the ego does not react, no further momentum is added to the karmic chapter, allowing it to close much faster.

What Is a High-Frequency Response to Prarabdha?

This brings us to our most important discussion: how does one create an intelligent or high-frequency response to karma? What is the nature of this response? Since karma can be a stepping stone to soul growth and maturity, real growth occurs only when we respond to it intelligently.

There are two aspects to this, so let us try to understand them.

1. An intelligent response to karma means we watch things as they unfold without investing emotionally, i.e., we don't create negative emotions in response. This means that when we realise we cannot change a person or a life situation, the first thing we do is protect ourselves. For it is in such moments that we are most vulnerable to the voice in our head, which repeatedly urges us to worry, stress, and be negative. Instead of giving in to the temporary pull of the

mind, we let a situation remain just a situation—not something that defines us. This happens when we withhold emotional energy from the situation.

Whenever we feel ourselves being drawn into emotional turmoil due to an external situation, we must learn to withdraw our attention from it. Even though our mind may want us to stay engaged—often exaggerating the situation and making it seem like a bigger deal than it actually is, through unnecessary and damaging narratives—it is precisely in such times that we must stop listening to the mind. We need to switch off our emotions and turn on our intelligence. This is vital because while karma brings the punishment, it is our emotions that build the prison, creating suffering. In such a state, we lose the awareness needed to positively influence our prarabdha.

Hence, choosing intelligence over emotions is crucial because none of us know where we may have faltered in the past, and none of us can avoid consequences. At some point, we must all face the results of our own deeds, as this is how we free ourselves from long-pending karmic debts. However, some people refuse to let go of negative experiences, replaying them repeatedly in their minds. Their emotions keep them bound to a negative karmic event or situation that should have ended once they faced the consequences of past actions. Yet, the more we invest emotionally in what we are going through, the more we remain prisoners of our own ignorant past. In this way, we never truly end karma because the more emotions we attach to a challenging prarabdha, the tighter our karmic knots become. Thus, even though a challenging prarabdha may cause hurt, we must not let hurt turn into suffering. This can only be achieved by not nourishing the hurt with our thoughts and emotions.

A question that arises here is: How can we gain control over our thoughts and emotions? The fact is that we cannot control our thoughts and emotions by trying to control them. If we attempt to control them, they only intensify. Instead, all we need to do is cultivate self-awareness: the process of watching our thoughts and emotions as they arise. Try to be a witness to them, and do not allow them to create a diminished version of the self. This is only possible when we remain as the awareness behind such thoughts and emotions, without extending the self beyond. The moment we start acting on negative thoughts and emotions, we become negative, further tightening the knots of karma. Therefore, we must hold on to that awareness and avoid identifying with negative thoughts and emotions.

2. An intelligent response to karma also means understanding that unfolding events and situations are part of life's experiences, meant to impart valuable lessons for our growth and maturity. With

this awareness, we must identify the areas of growth and maturity where we may be lacking. We need to examine the tendencies that karma is triggering in us and recognise that these tendencies are the seeds of everything unfolding externally.

Here, it is important to note that tendencies that consume us emotionally are not just from this life. While certain situations in this life may trigger them, they are rooted in the past. Anxiety, fear, anger, jealousy, or even depression, all are accumulations of many lifetimes, waiting to be addressed in the now.

For instance, if someone carries a lot of anger in their soul personality (whether active or passive), they will inevitably encounter people who trigger this anger. However, karmic closure with such individuals happens only when the anger transforms into peace within the person experiencing it. Similarly, if someone carries a deep-rooted fear, they will be confronted with situations that demand courage. Only when courage becomes an active part of their personality will these karmic situations either weaken or dissolve—otherwise, they will continue to repeat. Hence, intelligence lies in understanding what the karmic situation requires us to change within ourselves. And an intelligent response to karma means understanding that a difficult prarabdha is a call for self-transformation.

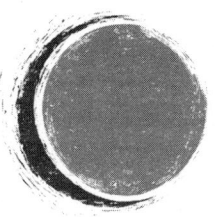

16

Ego: The Cause of Karma

'Karma means material action, that which is instigated by egoistic desire.'
—**Paramahansa Yogananda**

The night of the soul, which is the burden of karma, begins with the darkness of ego and ends with the light of wisdom. But the journey from darkness to light is a transformative one, starting with the understanding that ego is the cause of karma.

The ego arises when the real self becomes confused with the illusory and creates false identifications. This happens because, for the ego, there is nothing beyond the senses, beyond the physical realm or the world of forms. As a result, it amplifies our need to satisfy the senses and roots the self in the physical and the material. This attachment to the world of forms traps us in an endless cycle of desire. We constantly seek more, demand more, crave more approval, and long for more praise. In the process, what we fail to realise is that internally, we become less. Consequently, the mind becomes erratic, uneasy, restless, and constantly hungry for more. It also becomes fearful because it now depends on something that is easily changeable and temporary in nature. Thus, when any of the mind-created identifications are lost, one fears losing the self, their very identity, and their sense of belonging in the world. That is why the ego can be described as: **e**ase **g**ets **o**ver!

We must understand that ego is a state of misalignment, where we are misled and misdirected by being heavily invested in the world of forms while disconnected from our true spiritual self. Without a sense of who we truly are, we struggle when confronted with life's challenges, as they threaten our very existence and identity. And since struggle is a negative response to life, it complicates these challenges further, entangling us in karma. This struggle gives rise to deeper ignorance, leading to anger, fear, insecurity, jealousy, attachment, desires, greed, and low self-esteem. And since the ego drives us to operate through a false identity, the void within us deepens, and our sense of unease continues to grow. This is because the ego thrives on:

- Self-deception.
- A constant need to preserve all that we possess.
- The world's approval and self-worth derived from it.

As a result, we remain devoid of peace and self-acceptance, which is why ego is: ease gone away! An ego-driven person views life through misplaced notions that fuel their negative tendencies. When they interact with the world through these tendencies, the result is karma.

Ego, indeed, is the greatest flaw, as it is the master creator of all other negative tendencies like anger, fear, greed, vanity, and hate. And as for karma and destiny, they are not external forces but a consequence of our own personality, and if we find ourselves troubled by them, it is because we have an ego-driven personality. Therefore, it becomes imperative to investigate the ego, as only by getting rid of it can we stop energising karma and empower destiny.

So, let us address a few important questions about the ego to gain a deeper understanding of its nature and its impact on our lives.

1. What Is Ego?

Ego is an unhealthy accumulation of false identifications in our psyche that make us derive our sense of self from what is temporary rather than permanent, or in other terms, what is worldly rather than spiritual. In essence, ego is a disconnection from our true self, which is spiritual. It is a complete identification with concepts, beliefs, ideas, ideologies, objects, relationships, reference points, labels, situations, and narratives that belong to the material world and are not aligned with the spirit.

One may call such accumulation the conditioning of the mind, which makes us understand the self only in the context of worldly life. As a result, we feel a desperate need to cling to the experience of life and everything connected to it. This leads to a state where our external self feels bigger than our internal self. It compels us to invest in a larger-than-life image of ourselves in society or portray ourselves as something we are not. And even though this may bring temporary joy or pleasure to some, it neither leads to peace, happiness, or satisfaction nor does it empower consciousness.

2. How Does the Ego Operate?

The ego operates through conceptual and physical identification, shaping a narrative in the mind. Since it heavily identifies with forms, its narrative separates us from our true self—our spiritual self. This makes our spiritual personality, which embodies peace, happiness, love, purity, wisdom, compassion, freedom, humility, and power, less accessible, while our human personality, which embodies anger, hate, greed, lust, attachment, vanity, and fear, becomes more active. These vices are the primary tendencies through which the ego directs us, leading to their many subsets—criticism, doubt, judgement, comparison, dominance, control, low self-esteem, arrogance, obsession, compulsion, possessiveness, jealousy, anxiety, restlessness, pretentiousness, insecurity, defensiveness, oppression, and narcissism, among others. The energy of such tendencies is depleting compared to the tendencies aligned with the true nature of the spirit.

Furthermore, since the ego draws identity from everything worldly, it operates through concepts, beliefs, labels, and narratives, making us believe that our entire being and life's purpose are limited to the form. It does not allow us to recognise the self beyond the form (body) and the worldly roles we play through it. It does not let us realise that the role is merely an activity of the soul and not the soul itself. For it is the soul that energises the role and brings the form into action and interaction. But because we remain so heavily invested in these roles, we come to believe that they define us entirely, leading to even greater attachment to our form identity (physical self) and our role. And in its bid to make the role appear effective and impressive, the ego places greater emphasis on continuous form identifications, further fuelling tendencies that go against our spiritual nature.

Let's look at how our actions and perceptions are shaped by ego, influencing how we see ourselves and interact with the world.

i.   We aim to look better than others and constantly seek to please them through external appearance.

ii.   We fiercely protect our role-defined identity, whether as a woman, man, mother, parent, entrepreneur, doctor, etc.

iii. We become too attached to the role and everything associated with it.

iv. We show respect to labels and titles, and the bigger or fancier the label or title, the greater our respect for both others and ourselves. For example, a chauffeur receives less respect from us compared to a business tycoon.

v. We get hurt easily or engage in conflicts when our concepts, beliefs, or ideologies are challenged, or when our identity is threatened.

vi. We think endlessly because the ever-animated world of forms continuously fuels our mental narrative. So, regardless of how insignificant something is, we dwell on it.

vii. We cover up our own insecurities and preserve our worldly image through fake behaviour, lies, and hypocrisy.

viii. We strive for a sense of superiority because there is no equality in the world of forms. It operates on benchmarks that create a constant need to compete.

ix. We often compare or criticise others to derive this sense of superiority.

x. We love to discuss others, judging or evaluating both ourselves and others as either inferior or superior.

xi. We easily make enemies due to our biases.

xii. We become overly attached to relationships and possessions because we derive our sense of self from them.

xiii. We are constantly seeking more—more objects, titles, labels, power, control, money, and glorification through worldly attainments—because they provide us with a false sense of importance.

xiv. We seek importance because the world of forms relates to us through our status, which, again, is merely a label.

xv. We easily succumb to unhappiness or adopt a victim identity if we feel inferior compared to others or if the world fails to appreciate or acknowledge us.

xvi. We love to escape reality when the world feels difficult to handle—imagining scenarios that comfort our false sense of self or turning to sensory pleasures and addictions that distract us from difficulties that challenge our identity.

xvii. We become selfish and resort to extreme actions that violate our ethics and feed our greed.

xviii. We love to remain in the past or the future, ever disconnected from the present. The future feels more appealing because we believe it holds the promise of becoming something more, while the past remains a source of attachment because we fear losing the identity we have built from past experiences. The quality of these experiences does not matter; what matters is that an identity has been derived from them, and all energy is spent clinging to it.

xix. We relate to collective egos, which are far more dangerous than individual egos. This connection can be found anywhere—in political parties, spiritual organisations, religious groups, cults, communities, countries, societies, and even within families.

How Does Ego Create Karma?

Ego is the dominance of tendencies that negatively impact one's life. To understand how these lead to the creation of karma, we must examine how the ego influences our behaviour, choices, interactions, and responses to life. The same is discussed in the following points.

1. Loss of Powers

Ego results in the loss of inner power due to an incorrect identification of the self as merely the body rather than the soul. However, life is created only when a soul inhabits a form or body, meaning the soul holds greater power than the body. The body is impermanent and temporary, as is everything associated with ego identification. Our true identity is what is permanent—the soul. Yet, the ego convinces us that what is temporary is permanent. It operates through false identifications with objects, people, labels, and belief systems, preventing one from knowing the self beyond physical forms. This leads to an absence of soul consciousness and a heightened state of body consciousness. As a result, one's real identity is lost, along with the power to stay in control. Since emphasis remains solely on one's physical, sensory, mental, and emotional needs, dependency on the external world increases, allowing outside influences to dictate one's inner reality. The more disconnected we are from our spiritual identity, the more we seek validation from the external world. This leads to mental instability and a lack of peace—both key factors responsible for karma creation.

Soul consciousness, on the other hand, is a state of thoughtless awareness, i.e., one of peace, stillness, silence, and power, with minimal interference from the mind. In this state, the ability to discriminate between what is depleting and what is empowering, what is real and what is false, what is truth and what is illusion, is retained. This helps one engage with the world from a place of inner strength.

In contrast, body consciousness places the mind in complete control over a person. With excessive identification with the physical world, one's mind remains fuelled by mental narratives revolving around people and life situations. The power to make wise choices is lost in this internal noise, complicating life experiences and leading to actions driven by flawed energy, which in turn creates karma.

2. Disconnection from the Present Moment

Because the ego relies so heavily on thoughts, it prevents us from giving full attention to the present moment—the 'now'—where thoughts momentarily cease due to a temporary disconnection from the past or future. Being in the now means focusing entirely on what is. However, since the ego needs the past and future to construct narratives about what was or what could be, it resists the present. The ego clings to the misery or glory of the past because it reinforces a conceptual identity. It also cannot stop worrying about or dreaming of the future, as the future either poses a threat or offers the hope of a better identity.

Thus, being fully present is uncomfortable for the ego, as it leaves little room for thought, and therefore, no stress, worry, fear, or anxiety, meaning no actions bound by karma. And since life always exists in the now—in what is, not in what was or what could be—the ego misaligns us with reality, creating disharmony with life. This misalignment leads to flawed energy exchanges with the world, resulting in karma.

3. Fear

Since the ego heavily identifies with what's worldly and keeps us in the past or the future, it energises fear—fear of not being enough, fear of what others will think or say, fear of what's to come, even fear of failure and disappointment, and fear of losing someone or something. Fear destroys our spontaneity and confidence, resulting in self-doubt and lack of self-esteem.

Our fear and doubts also don't let us invest in others because when we doubt the self, we also don't trust others. We either judge and criticise others, or we overdo things for them to please them and win their appreciation. The result of such actions is a sense of weariness and anxiety, which eventually converts into karmic complications. In certain cases, low self-esteem makes one a bully, a narcissist, or someone so full of oneself (due to insecurity) that they control and offend others.

So, fear means our energy remains so heavy that others begin to feel uncomfortable with us. They either resist us or reject us altogether. And that is how the most complex karmic accounts get created.

4. Anger

Ego causes anger because, with ego, we strongly identify with our beliefs. There is no room for adjustment, compromise, flexibility, or letting go. Anger arises when there is a clash between reality and expectations, i.e., when situations or people do not respond in accordance with our mental concepts or narratives about them or their behaviour.

Anger is not just the outcome of egoic behaviour; it is also the weapon the ego uses to gain control of what is slipping out of one's hands. Sadness, judgement, blame, hurt, hate, conflict, struggle, derision, pain, and misery—which lead to the creation of karma—are all forms of anger.

5. Attachments

Attachment is another form of ego, which arises due to excessive identification with something that gives us our sense of self. It means an emotional connection to people, possessions, places, or even experiences, with the belief that they are a part of us. And we suffer because we are unable to see the self as separate from them, so the slightest change or disturbance to these aspects tends to destabilise us.

Attachment is the illusion of 'me' and 'mine', which manifests as excessive dependency or a sense of ownership and entitlement toward everyone and everything we are emotionally and selfishly invested in—selfishly because we derive our sense of self through those very relationships or things. Without them, we feel incomplete or less, and so, whether it is our family, friends, work, status, possessions, or labels, we are always heavily guarded toward them. This leads to an unfair bias and a lack of freedom and space in life and relationships, causing suffocation and emotional turmoil, which contribute to karma creation in relationships.

6. Overthinking

A thought may not have any consequences, but thinking is incessant thoughts, which drain us. Excessive thoughts build mental drama and make us lose energy, the result of which is stress. And since ego relies on overthinking—which means continuous mental stories around forms—stress is the natural outcome.

Our ego also suppresses intuition, and the route it takes is through the mind. Intuition is lost in the noise of the mind. And without the necessary guidance from our intuition, we are bound to feel lost. Also, overthinking, which is the ego's favourite activity, is often due to poor-quality thoughts, which increase the speed of thinking. These further contribute to stress and negativity. Our negative thoughts feed negative emotions, and from such a state, we neither attract anything positive nor do our interactions yield the right results.

To conclude, our ego gets hardened with the extensive use of all such egoic tendencies, as mentioned above. And since we remain ignorant about the ego, we continue operating through such tendencies. Thus, we remain stuck in the psychological realm of the ego.

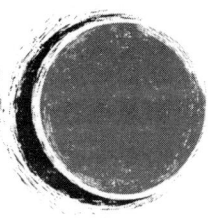

17

Karmic Settlement in the Bhagavad Gita

Since ancient times, karma has been one of the most intriguing subjects for religious intellectuals, enlightened beings, and ordinary people alike. The understanding of this concept has evolved over time, but the most ancient spiritual text that introduced us to the idea of karma is the 'Bhagavad Gita'—a book that is part of the Indian epic *Mahabharata*. The Gita transcends time and age, serving as a textual guide filled with divine wisdom to help one attain higher consciousness. Within this book lies the greatest secret to karmic settlement, offering timeless wisdom to souls who feel lost and overwhelmed by karmic challenges. Passed down by a divine being (Lord Krishna) to a great warrior (Arjuna), this knowledge serves as a guiding light for all.

In his guidance to Arjuna, Lord Krishna reveals that the root of all weakness and evil—the very source of karma—

is the ego. He explains that true liberation comes not from battling karma but from confronting and dissolving its very source, ultimately bringing an end to karma itself. As the legend goes, during the battle of *Mahabharata*, Arjuna experiences an extreme psychological conflict. He is torn between his duty to fight for what is just and his attachment to his own family, whom he must battle. Unable to raise arms against his own kin, Arjuna grapples with the dilemma of engaging in a war that will ultimately result in their deaths. His ego—manifesting as ignorance, attachment, and fear—stands in the way of his duty: to take righteous action and honour his valour, a rare gift of this invincible warrior.

Arjuna's fear stems from the belief that he will be committing a sin. His attachment binds him to those he deeply identifies as his own, and his ignorance prevents him from seeing beyond the world of forms. His consciousness is heavily identified with the material world, its labels (relationships), and emotional traps. As a result, he remains oblivious to the spiritual truth and considers the material world, with all its good and evil, as something he cannot afford to lose. This is typical of a man bound by ego—who is unable to recognise that the consequences of his deeds are attached to the soul. Since the ego opposes the soul, Arjuna is unable to fight against evil. His attachment to his loved ones (regardless of their deeds) and his fear of losing them blind him to wisdom, making this great warrior reluctant to confront the forces of darkness and combat evil.

Here, evil refers to the humiliation and dishonour suffered by Draupadi at the hands of Arjuna's own blood relations. Those who perpetrated this sin were meant to be fought and defeated in the ensuing battle. Since Draupadi was publicly shamed by them, the entire premise of the battle of *Mahabharata* was the settlement of a karmic debt that Arjuna, as her husband, and the Pandavas, his true brothers, owed to Draupadi. Moreover, having been both the primary cause of her misery and humiliation and passive spectators to her exploitation at the hands of their cousin Duryodhana, the Pandavas were equally guilty of the sin. For this, they had to settle a heavy karmic debt.

The root cause of the conflict between the Pandavas and their relatives, the Kauravas, was individual ego. In the Kauravas, it manifested as arrogance, greed, lust, and anger, ultimately leading to this epic battle. So, as Arjuna stood in the battlefield, lost between ignorance, dilemma, and duty, Lord Krishna intervened and shook him out of his egoic slumber, awakening him to the truth that had eluded his memory—the truth of his identity as the soul that creates karma by failing to fight evil and stand up for what is right.

Notably, Krishna does not offer Arjuna an external remedy, ritual, or motivational speech. Instead, he urges him not to be a coward but to confront and defeat his inner demons so that he may fight the battle. In Krishna's words: 'O son of Prtha, do not be dissuaded by this weakness of spirit. Vanquisher of enemies, shed this impotency and get ready to fight.' Krishna reveals to Arjuna how his ego creates delusions that weaken his spirit and make him reluctant to fight against evil.

Another significant aspect is that Lord Krishna does not fight the war for Arjuna. Though he could have singlehandedly won the battle for the Pandavas, he entered the battlefield with the precondition that he would not fight for either side. This was because the pending karma belonged to Arjuna and the Pandavas, and they had to settle it themselves. The divine could only intervene through wisdom, not action—an eternal principle of the law of karma, common to all mankind. Thus, the only way forward for Arjuna and the Pandavas was to fight—not just to punish the guilty but also to restore the dignity and trust of their wife, Draupadi. This was their karmic mandate, and divine consciousness was willing to guide them toward what was fair and right. However, wisdom was neither imposed on Arjuna nor was he compelled in any way. He had free will to understand and apply the wisdom that would ultimately lead him to the right state of mind and, consequently, the right action.

Therefore, we can see that Krishna's wisdom was a call to self-discovery and action. It revolved around three key aspects that define human character and conduct. These are:

1. **Dharma:** A pure, righteous, and elevated inner state leading to meaningful action.
2. **Adharma:** An egoic state leading to ignorance, illusions, and destructive action.

3. **Swadharma:** A state determined by one's individual strengths, latent gifts, and talents, leading to the fulfilment of one's duty and life purpose.

Dharma is action driven by truth and purity of intention. *Adharma* is corrupt or egoic action. *Swadharma* includes actions one is born to fulfil and must be directed toward the greater good while also honouring one's karmic duty. Yet, before taking any action, Arjuna had an even greater task: to become self-aware in the light of truth and dissolve the tendencies that empowered his ego, turning a great warrior into a self-doubting, weak, and confused man. And so, the battle that Krishna initiated for Arjuna was not against his external enemies but against the tendencies that strengthened his ego.

Thus, it is important to recognise that Krishna's message was not to motivate Arjuna to kill his own relatives but to awaken dharma within his consciousness so that he could fight adharma and settle his pending karma. However, Arjuna could only do this if his ego did not stand in the way of his swadharma (his duty). This understanding is what Lord Krishna imparts to Arjuna as he seeks to remove the veil of ego, or *maya,* and awaken the great warrior to the true mandate of his life.

The term maya in Hindu philosophy does not simply mean materiality or the world of forms. Maya is the play of ego, which negates our spiritual truth and heavily identifies with the illusory aspects of the material world. It separates us from our spiritual or higher self, which is connected to dharma, or righteousness. Maya keeps us trapped in worldly illusions, leading to adharma. Therefore, the wisdom of the Gita is centred on the psychological warfare between dharma and adharma, aiming to help human consciousness see through the illusions of maya.

In simple terms, Krishna's message to Arjuna was this: If you cannot look beyond the ego (the veil of maya), you cannot understand swadharma (your duty), which is to restore dharma (what is right). And if you are unable to restore dharma, you cannot settle karma.

The great rishi (sage) Ved Vyasa, who narrated this ancient text, aimed for the restoration of dharma. Since the text was conceived and created in superconsciousness (heightened awareness), he understood that when humans lose their inner paradise—their spiritual powers—to their ego, they become burdened with heavier debts of karma. And to dissolve such debts, humans must first battle their own ignorance (ego). Thus, Kurukshetra, the battleground of the *Mahabharata*, represents the life situations that challenge us to confront our ego and reinstate dharma.

And so, the reality of the *Mahabharata* holds profound relevance for all of us trapped in the cycle of birth, death, and karma. Arjuna represents those who struggle between ego and true duty, just as we do in our own lives. Our body is like a chariot, carrying us into the world of forms to resolve unfinished karma, while life itself is the battlefield of Kurukshetra, where we must transcend the ego and restore dharma to break free from karma. Each birth is a soul's journey into this battleground, seeking the wisdom needed to conquer the ego, manifested through various behavioural tendencies that fuel karma. But only a soul that becomes a seeker of wisdom (Arjuna), regardless of its form-identified caste, creed, religion, geography, or gender, can understand the true purpose of life, which is to dissolve the ego, and with it, bring an end to karma and restore dharma.

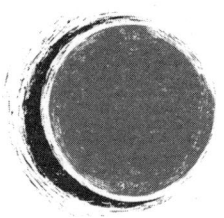

18

Ego Awareness

The ego is often an accumulation of many lives, which gets reflected in our conditioned response to life. These responses tend to be less original, lacking self-awareness, and driven more by reaction than conscious choice. The ego is also a reflection of the world—its concepts, ideologies, beliefs, preferences, choices, aspirations, practices, and thoughts—because it makes us heavily identify with the world.

Since we have lived before and will live again, an important question that helps create awareness of the ego is: Have we lived well and to our full capacity? Have we understood the self in the context of this existence? Have we loved ourselves and our life enough? Or are we merely existing, struggling, surviving, questioning, complaining, and carrying on year after year, life after life? If the latter is true, then we are heavily influenced by the ego. But here is the googly—the same situation may imply that we are closer to dissolving our ego. Seems counterintuitive, right? Let's explore this further.

All suffering results from our own internal response to an external situation, using fear, anger, hurt, attachments, and desires. This response is the natural outcome of our dependence on the external world, false identifications, misleading beliefs, and illusory concepts. At the core of it all is the conditioning of our ego, which distorts our perception and keeps us trapped in these cycles. So, when every life situation, event, and equation is seen through the filter of ego, we lose our innate ability to create our own peace and happiness. We begin to rely on others or the external world for the same, as our ego-identified self is incapable of creating peace and happiness. It seeks power in everything external.

But it is important to realise that the external world is transient and unpredictable. And so, our state of peace and happiness keeps changing in accordance with it. Like the moon, we exist in phases—waxing and waning. This means there are also times of complete darkness which bring grief, emotional pain, and suffering so deep that we are compelled to seek answers to the mystery of life's problems. Any such seeking is the beginning of the end of the ego. In other words, the awareness of the discomfort created by the ego marks the beginning of its dissolution. So, it is suffering at the hands of the ego that makes us surrender to the light of wisdom, and wisdom creates awareness of the ego.

The *Mahabharata* also highlights this, as Arjuna, who represents all of humanity, becomes so overwhelmed by life's dilemmas that he is compelled to seek deeper understanding. In this moment of vulnerability, wisdom—embodied by Lord Krishna—comes to his aid, guiding him toward clarity and truth. This great epic also depicts the plight of those who, under the influence of ego—manifested as greed, vanity, anger, and jealousy—commit grave mistakes that ultimately lead to their downfall and destruction. Such was the karmic fate of the Pandavas' warring brothers, the Kauravas, who earned their own ruin through misdeeds.

Given the nature of life, anyone can find themselves in a situation like Arjuna's or the Pandavas', who, despite being good humans, lost their direction and succumbed to evil at a moment of grave human weakness. Their tragedy unfolded in the courtroom of Hastinapur, where mistakes made under the influence of egoistic tendencies led to the most serious karmic implications. The *Mahabharata* thus highlights two specific kinds of ego: one embodied by Arjuna, representing all the Pandavas, and the other by Duryodhana, representing the Kauravas. Let's look at the key differences between these two forms of ego.

Duryodhana's is a hardened ego, and it is more damaging because it leaves little room for wisdom. It invites suffering through resistance to change. This kind of ego is common among those who are self-destructive and destined to pay a heavy price. Their spiritual growth can only come through the harshest lessons of life, as they resist wisdom rather than embrace it.

In such cases, the ego makes one believe:

1. I know everything!
2. I am above all!
3. I can destroy!
4. I want! (Not out of need, but greed.)
5. I need control!

On the other hand, Arjuna has a softer ego. Meaning, this ego is less dominant and less destructive and is often common among those who feel lost due to excessive emotions and attachments. This type of ego clings to form identification out of a sense of goodness and the intention to protect, preserve, and avoid destruction. Such individuals are more willing to confront their confusion, pain, and fear. They remain open to the wisdom that can guide them out of misery.

This ego is more about:

1. I am lost.
2. I am not enough.
3. I am a victim.
4. I am insecure.
5. I fear.

It is also important to note here that ego manifests in these two ways within all of us. Depending on our intention—whether to destroy or to preserve—it either attracts destruction through suffering or awakening through wisdom despite initial suffering.

Ultimately, to overcome the ego, we must first become uncomfortable with it. This is because only extreme discomfort caused by the ego can shake our ignorance and compel us to seek answers—answers that bring the necessary wisdom to make us aware of the ego. And it is this awareness that leads to realisation, which, in turn, sparks transformation, allowing one to perceive life through the lens of wisdom rather than ego.

In *Mahabharata*, Lord Krishna's role as Arjuna's charioteer depicts the same. The chariot symbolises Arjuna's journey from ignorance to light. His suffering—born of illusions, attachments, and fear—cracks open his ego, creating an opening for wisdom to enter. This leads to greater self-awareness and the realisation of truth, marking the beginning of the end of his ego. Thus, we can conclude that the true antidote to ego is the awakening of inner wisdom. It ensures that the good in all of us ultimately triumphs over evil. And in Arjuna's transformation, there is a greater message for all of mankind, troubled by varying degrees of the ego.

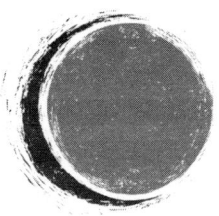

19

The End of Ego and Karma

'When there is no "I" there is no karma.'
—Ramana Maharshi

As we have discussed, karma results from ego-driven behaviour. So, the end of karma means the end of ego and a return to our higher self. However, the journey from our conditioned, ego-driven self to our highest, spiritual self is both challenging and arduous. Wisdom is the bridge that connects these two states, transforming ignorance into awakening and, ultimately, enlightenment. Yet, shedding the ego and awakening to our higher self is a gradual process with many facets. Let us explore some of the key aspects of this journey.

1. Correct Identification

Since the ego's world revolves around concepts tied to the world of forms, leading to illusions of me and mine, the first step needed is to transcend these identifications. This does not mean completely disconnecting from who and what we have known the self to be. Rather, it means recognising the self and others correctly—as beings in human form—and realising the temporary nature of forms alongside the permanence of the being. And only when we understand who we truly are—spiritual beings navigating a human experience—does the ego lose its power. This realisation shifts control from the form to the spirit. We recognise that while the spirit is eternal, it merely inhabits a physical form during its human journey. We also come to see that everything in the world of forms is temporary, bringing about a shift in consciousness. Understanding the transient nature of the material world releases emotional dependency on it, leading to freedom from fear, attachment, greed, and egoistic connections that entangle one in karma.

Remember, the ego needs everything worldly to survive. It clings to worldly labels that provide a temporary and false sense of identity. And when our ego-led consciousness is invested in labels, we engage in comparisons and judgements, which become primary sources of unhappiness and anxiety. The more we identify the self as the body or the form, the more we remain trapped in labels of relationships, caste, religion, rank, designation, status, geography, and so on. This means we measure the value and merit of ourselves and others on the scale of what is transient and worldly. Such identification causes negative behaviours—comparison, insecurity, criticism, complaining, and judgement—further entrenching us in ego and karma. Moreover, when we view the world through form identification—also known as body consciousness—we miss the bigger picture. We lose our sense of oneness with other souls and overlook their long journeys and connections across lifetimes. This is why we fail to grasp karma and its implications. We do not recognise the power of our deeds and their consequences, which sustain soul connections in human life through karma.

The fact is that when everything is reduced to the body, life's scope appears limited. What matters most is maximising personal gain in all interactions— seeking maximum control, pleasure, comfort, attachments, and all that reinforces a sense of security and worth. Such an approach to life generates negative karma, leading to suffering. Yet, when we suffer, we complain, get angry, feel hurt and resentful, and blame others or life itself for our misery. This happens because we view life only through forms, which complicates matters, making us unable to see how our tendencies shape life and its interactions. Without self-responsibility, accountability, or awareness of our own role in suffering, we remain trapped in a cycle of ignorance. However, when we begin to recognise our ignorance—wrapped in form-identified labels—we start to see from a higher perspective. Our spiritual reality creates freedom from all labels and fosters a sense of oneness with all beings. In this state, neither ego nor karma can exist.

Here, it is important to understand that the ego cannot survive without attachments, fear, greed, vanity, lust, and anger. All these tendencies arise because our consciousness is overly identified with the body. And since the body is subject to change, we remain ever insecure. The limitations of form create chaos in our psyche, making us fear loss, cling to people and things, crave more and want it faster, and react with anger when our expectations aren't met. This is the chaos on which the ego thrives. But when our consciousness is aligned correctly, we understand the self and others as eternal beings with nothing to lose or gain—except spiritual power. This shift in awareness changes our perspective on life and people, opening us to the understanding and acceptance of soul connections. Life and relationships gain depth as we realise these connections are not bound by time or labels. There is more to them, and to us, than what we have known through our ego-identified self. We come to see that our life experiences are shaped by our soul personality, developed over multiple lifetimes. And if an experience is unpleasant, it signals the need for self-correction. Such understanding raises self-awareness and creates deeper empathy for others, and acceptance of past mistakes that may be causing present karmic suffering.

Thus, as we transition from body or ego consciousness to soul consciousness, we embark on the journey toward our higher self. In doing so, we begin to respond to life in ways that dissolve karma and free us from further bondage. We realise that we are not the body but the soul or pure energy. And this energy is our ultimate reality. It defines who we are, shapes our karmic history, and determines how the world relates to us. It influences how people feel about us, the experiences we attract, and the environment we create within and around us. Through our thoughts, emotions, and interactions, this energy forms the very field through which we connect with others.

This shift in awareness helps dissolve karma by:

1. A deeper connection with the self and all life.

2. A sense of oneness builds greater acceptance and the understanding that our shared past with people and situations is interconnected, not separate from our present.

3. Freedom from fear, arising from the realisation that we are eternal and that our journey continues beyond the body.

2. Unlearning

Unlearning is an incredibly important part of consciousness evolution. Unless we unlearn certain deeply embedded aspects of our psyche—the very roots of our conditioning—we cannot adopt a new way of looking at life. A way that allows us to mature, evolve, and live through our higher self.

The fact is that everything we have learnt so far shapes our thought process, belief system, life concepts, understanding of the self and others, and even our perception of the universe and God. The way we relate to the world and to ourselves stems from this learning or conditioning. Every time we need to define something about life or the self, we access this conditioning, which in turn influences how we relate to the world and to ourselves. So, we are conditioned to respond and interact in specific ways.

Furthermore, our conditioning is largely determined by what is stored in our soul memory as recordings. The tendencies most dominant in our personality—those we have used most actively—form a major part of these recordings, developed over different forms and lifetimes. And with egoistic tendencies dominant in our personality, it is likely that we have learnt the wrong things along the way and have been conditioned in a way that nurtures the ego. Breaking such conditioning is essential for dissolving the ego, as it acts like a wall that prevents wisdom from entering—a wall that safeguards old habits, thought patterns, feelings, belief systems, and conceptual identifications.

It is also crucial to understand that conditioning is always of the mind. The mind, led by the ego, clings to whatever sustains the ego. Therefore, the mind must unlearn. Unlearning is crucial to dissolving egoistic conditioning, as only by shedding the old can the ego be weakened.

But what do we mean by 'unlearning'? Let's take a closer look at its true meaning.

- Unlearning is the non-identification with form-based concepts, belief systems, responses, choices, and preferences that keep the ego active.

- Unlearning is letting go of the mental narrative about the self and others that originate from stored memory or information solely focused on forms.

- Unlearning is resisting the impulses of habitual thinking and questioning what we have learnt and understood so far.

- Unlearning is consciously shifting how we think and perceive by experimenting with wisdom and allowing it to reshape our thoughts, beliefs, and concepts.

- Unlearning is starting afresh, exploring new and more self-empowering ideas, and integrating them into our way of life.

- Unlearning is disbelieving any information that instils fear.

Therefore, we can say that unlearning is the most powerful way to break the momentum of the ego. But why is this process so challenging and time-consuming? Even when considering just a single lifetime, conditioning occurs in countless ways. From the energy received in the mother's womb to the formative years of life, from parental and genetic influences to societal and cultural environments, and from traditions to the kind of knowledge one is exposed to—each of these factors shapes our conditioning. This conditioning only strengthens as we age. And because we are deeply affected by our immediate environment, we emulate what we see around us. In the process, we lose our originality and uniqueness. Additionally, reprogramming one's consciousness is often met with strong resistance from emotions tied to long-standing conditioning, especially when this conditioning spans not just one lifetime but many. In fact, every soul carries an entire database of stored learning that must be unloaded or dropped altogether before it can absorb new information and reprogram itself accordingly.

The benefit of unlearning is that it ensures inner advancement by making way for something new. Without unlearning, we cannot let go of the past and create space for growth. Therefore, to unlearn and start afresh, we need to inquire, observe, assess, gather new information, and experiment with different ways of being and living. It is equally important to be honest with ourselves and discipline the mind, ensuring it does not cling rigidly to old behavioural patterns, concepts, and beliefs. This is how unlearning begins. And the more we familiarise ourselves with something new or recognise its power, the easier it becomes to unlearn the old.

The importance of redefining oneself and letting go of the old is underscored by the fact that repetitive patterns prevent spiritual evolution. As creatures of habit, we often become engaged in the old in ways that lead to stagnation and boredom. However, anyone who recognises the danger of such a state will naturally seek renewal. And anyone open to change—anyone striving to create a better version of themselves—will find joy and excitement in learning something new while unlearning the old.

The willingness to unlearn also sends the right message to the universe—a message of readiness and openness, free from attachment to comfort and habitual patterns. This, in turn, attracts the wisdom and guidance necessary to step beyond the ego. And because openness to change is an act of fearlessness, it signals the end of the ego.

3. **Working Against the Ego**

    Start by recognising the ego as this breaks its momentum. When your emotions are fuelled by anger, fear, attachment, arrogance, or resentment, or when you feel superior or inferior to others, know that the ego has taken over. Be aware.

    The ego loves the comfort zone. It craves familiarity and praise and takes criticism too seriously. This is why challenging the ego is important. This can be done by being self-assured and confident, accepting others' opinions without being defined by them, and not seeing yourself through their perspective. This helps break the ego's hold. So does surrounding yourself with people who have a different vibe—the kind that makes you uncomfortable but also teaches you valuable lessons about human behaviour. The kind of vibe that is necessary for inner growth, strength, depth, and maturity because it pushes your limits of understanding, acceptance, and adjustment. This, in turn, helps you evolve through patience, forgiveness, endurance, and compassion—all positive qualities that empower the soul and dissolve the ego.

Here are a few things that must be avoided, as they inflate the ego and build negative karma:

1. Criticism: It makes our energy complex, heavy, and difficult to handle.

2. Comparisons: They lower self-esteem, slow us down, and cause underperformance in important areas of life, leading to loss and anxiety.

3. Confusion: It traps us in a battle between the mind and intellect, resulting in stress.

4. Negative reactions: They create inner turbulence and a negatively charged personality.

5. Pointless discussions: They drain us and cause emotional turmoil.

6. Endless expectations: They keep us on edge and deepen the sense of emptiness.

Beyond this, the ego's favourite tendency is anger. Anger creates hurt, and hurt is karmic. Therefore, we must make an effort not to use or hold onto anger. We cannot remove anger simply by deciding to get rid of it; we can only overcome it by cultivating peace. The more we live in peace, the more peaceful we become. And it is this inner peace that eventually leaves no room for anger.

It is also important not to empower anger or hurt through additional thoughts and feelings. Instead, we must shift to awareness consciousness, which means knowing without becoming what we know and understanding what is harmful. This means that while we remain aware of our anger and hurt, we do not operate through them. Nor do we create additional thoughts that fuel negative emotions. And over time, through greater self-awareness and non-identification, we can transcend anger and hurt. This may not happen immediately, but with consistent practice, we gradually grow more peaceful and healed.

So, if you recognise the need to work on your ego, simply learn to observe your egoic tendencies as a detached witness. Do not attach emotions to them or identify yourself through them. Gradually, replace them with the qualities of your spiritual nature. For when we cease responding to the ego-driven self, we naturally begin to move beyond the ego.

4. Greater Self-awareness

Our level of self-awareness determines whether we are victims or in control of life. Only through self-awareness can we understand the damage caused by the ego and choose the right tendencies to bring into our behaviour. Only through self-awareness can we break old habitual patterns and conditioning and enter a field of higher vibration, which is conducive to ending karma.

Therefore, a greater degree of self-awareness becomes essential—awareness of how we interact with others and engage with life. A lack of self-awareness complicates life. Here's how:

1. When we aren't self-aware, we become consumed by mental noise. We easily burden and drain our minds through overthinking, overanalysing, and over-assessing life, people, and situations. This makes us anxious and restless and can also turn karmic, especially if our thoughts are negative. Negative thoughts, when they take over our psyche, colour our feelings with darkness.

2. A lack of self-awareness leads to a lack of attention toward the self. This can easily draw us into the tension of the collective consciousness, which is largely stressed, anxious, and fearful.

3. Without self-awareness, we live ignorantly and are controlled by the ego.

To cultivate awareness, one must understand that the mind and awareness are separate. Through awareness, we can probe the mind and identify egoic patterns. We can observe our behaviour and our responses to life. While one may be ignorantly and compulsively led by the mind, with awareness one becomes an observer of the mind. This helps in understanding the ego, as the ego operates through the mind. So, in our interactions with life, we must remain deeply aware of ourselves, which includes our thoughts, feelings, emotions, and inner responses.

To conclude this point, let's briefly explore the importance of greater self-awareness.

1. Self-awareness helps us see beyond our mental projections and the limited beliefs of the ego. It enables us to understand our own mind, which is necessary to grasp the play of the ego.

2. Through self-awareness, we can gain an unbiased perspective of our strengths and weaknesses and learn from occasional mistakes.

3. Self-awareness brings clarity, which is essential for dissolving ego-induced fear.

4. It allows us to take better control of life rather than being compulsively led by the mind.

5. With self-awareness, we know when, where, and how to change as individuals.

6. It exposes what is false and damaging and brings us closer to the truth—our spiritual nature.

7. Self-awareness enables us to live consciously, rather than ignorantly.

8. It shifts our focus from karmic suffering to the cause of suffering, helping us recognise the pointlessness of suffering.

9. Self-awareness replaces suffering with a continuous process of learning and evolving, without which the ego cannot be eliminated.

5. Embracing Wisdom

It is true that life is neither random nor arbitrary. Everything is in order. Everything is as it should be. Good or bad is just a label. And so, we get what we create. In other words, we create our own life. What returns is karma, and it returns with the same energy with which it was created. Whether this energy is challenging or a humbling and enlightening experience depends on the state of one's consciousness, as the energy of karma takes on the colour of one's consciousness. When consciousness evolves, the experience of karma becomes a path to enlightenment rather than suffering. This evolution occurs through wisdom, as higher wisdom dissolves ignorance—the very foundation of egoistic conditioning.

Wisdom is more essential than ever, as anger, stress, and worry have become so normalised that they seem inseparable from our existence. In fact, the way we function today, these emotions seem like all there is to us and have become embedded in the collective consciousness. Given our ego, we tend to get hurt or offended easily or become too attached to people, labels, and things. Terminologies such as 'ego is important', 'my ego cannot accept this', 'they hurt my ego', and 'it is important to have some ego' are commonplace. However, by saying such things, we naturally identify with and defend the ego.

So, to break free from this ignorance and develop true discernment of what is right and what is not, wisdom is indispensable. Let's explore some key ways in which wisdom guides us:

1. Wisdom helps us become self-aware.
2. Wisdom helps us introspect and distinguish between what is egoistic and what is spiritual.
3. Wisdom helps us alter our ego-identified reference points and outlook on life.
4. Wisdom helps us redefine our approach, attitude, perspective, and response to life in ways that make experiences more positive.
5. Wisdom helps us understand the bigger picture, settle our karmic debts uncomplainingly, reduce our burden of karma, and expedite the journey to spiritual growth.
6. Wisdom helps us break free from the trappings of the ego.

Since our ego is built over many lifetimes, we need wisdom to dissolve it, as wisdom helps us understand the true nature and cause of the ego, which varies from person to person. With wisdom, all solutions to the ego become possible. Thus, the only way out of the ego is by embracing wisdom.

6. Spiritual Growth

Most of our suffering in life stems not from situations themselves but from our lack of acceptance of what is. Since resistance is the play of the ego, as long as we continue responding to life through the ego, we continue to suffer.

Spiritual growth is the only way to end the play of the ego. But it can be achieved only by responding to life through the virtues of the spirit, not the vices of the ego. And until we interact with life through our spiritual nature—peace, love, happiness, wisdom, courage, compassion, humility, and purity—spiritual growth eludes us, and the ego continues to keep us trapped in karmic complexities. And so, for the ego to dissolve, our spiritual nature must reflect in our behaviour—this is real growth. However, spiritual growth does not occur overnight. It unfolds in stages, gradually transforming human consciousness by peeling away layers of the ego, a process that takes time.

Typically, the nine stages of spiritual growth include:

1. Extreme suffering that leads to asking the necessary questions about life.
2. Seeking answers to understand the cause of suffering.
3. Engaging in higher wisdom.
4. Higher self-awareness through wisdom, leading to an understanding of the ego.
5. A moment of awakening that brings a realisation of the self-sabotaging ways of the ego.
6. A desire to change and step out of the ego.
7. Effort to dissolve the ego through wisdom.
8. A shift in consciousness, leading to the removal of the ego.
9. Spiritual growth or realignment with our higher self.

To conclude, our spiritual growth ultimately leads to the dissolution of the ego, as the higher purpose of human life is to realign with our spiritual nature, where the ego loses all power and control, and one attains liberation. Liberation not only from unhealthy behaviour but also from its consequences, which return as karma. Thus, the end of karma begins only with the dissolution of the ego.

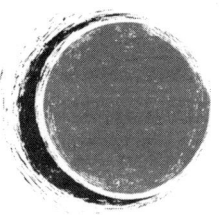

20

Identifying Pending Karma

Life revolves around the axis of our pending karma. The majority of what is pending stems from the past, playing its part in the present and manifesting as a debt. But this debt includes not only experiences we must go through as consequences of past deeds but also the tendencies responsible for them, which must be transformed. This transformation is equally important in settling the debt.

But how does one know what is pending? Is it a reward or an experience meant to challenge our ego? To answer this, we must become impartial observers, striving to understand life and ourselves from a deeper perspective. This helps identify areas of life with unresolved karma.

To start with, here is what we can do:

1. Pay attention to our own tendencies while interacting in life.

2. Try to understand whether a situation is triggering an egoistic response in us.

3. Decipher the nature of the situation.

4. Identify areas of difficulty or aspects of life that demand a lot from us. For example, situations that push us toward growth but also meet stiff resistance from us.

It is also essential to note that pending karma varies from person to person because each individual has a unique past and a distinct character and is travelling at a different pace of spiritual evolution and growth. So, even if one gains the right insights in the quest to understand pending karma, some aspects will always remain unrevealed.

In other words, karma cannot be summed up in a few points. But let us try to understand how pending karma can be identified through some scenarios.

- **Scenario 1**

  As we have discussed, a hardened ego often signals a heavy burden of pending karma. And just as financial debt or an unpaid loan keeps us restless until it is settled, a heavy karmic burden creates persistent anxiety, often without a clear reason that the conscious mind can assess. But understanding that, as souls, we all carry subtle memories—and that these memories manifest through tendencies—is helpful in assessing our pending karma. This is especially true because our unhealed parts surface as doubts, jealousy, anger, fear, attachment, insecurity, vanity, and greed, indicating a hardened ego and a heavy burden of pending karma.

When the subconscious carries a heavy recording of karmic debts, it may manifest in the following ways:

1. A persistent sense of restlessness, edginess, or anxiety for no apparent reason.
2. A tendency to overthink or overanalyse everything.
3. Disturbed sleep or frequent dreams.
4. Difficulty in accessing stillness.
5. Discomfort with silence.
6. Deep-seated trust issues and unaddressed fears.

What is important to understand here is that it is our conscience that writes our karmic script. Our conscience acts as an inner magistrate, ensuring that we do not escape our lessons and growth. These lessons unfold through karmic experiences, creating an environment for restoration, reformation, and transformation of consciousness.

- **Scenario 2**

A difficult life marked by constant challenges, setbacks, failures, or losses indicates that one is settling major karmic debts. However, such a life is not necessarily a punishment. It is, in fact, a means to expedite spiritual progress and attain freedom from a significant portion of pending karma. Meaning, that if the soul bravely endures its journey without complaint and faces challenges as they come, it suggests that the ego is not dominant, and the spirit is strong and ready to evolve. In such cases, this life could be the soul's own choice—a path to attain freedom and growth, driven by a deep yearning for spiritual evolution. Thus, we can conclude that since karma acts as both a hurdle and a roadblock to spiritual growth, some souls may choose to settle a heavier balance of pending karmas in a single lifetime to accelerate their evolution. And since karma brings valuable lessons, these souls gain a deeper understanding through their experiences.

- **Scenario 3**

The rules of karmic law are simple. Those who judge others will be judged. Those who do not accept others as they are may face rejection. Those who criticise others will remain peaceless. Put simply, karma spares no one and largely helps us evolve through our mistakes.

Though at times in life, we may recognise the mistakes we have made and understand their consequences. And when we fully realise the cause, facing the results becomes easier. However, there are also times when we encounter negative events, situations, or experiences and suffer without knowing why. This can be painful, as we find ourselves clueless, questioning life, and unable to understand why things are happening the way they are. This is the karma of previous lifetimes. And since our memory cannot trace the mistakes, we feel lost and overwhelmed.

So, the main takeaway here is that in both cases, there was a mistake—in one, we remember it, and in the other, we have forgotten.

- **Scenario 4**

Hate, anger, jealousy, insecurity, and fear are strong emotions that often bind us to the very people for whom we harbour such feelings. These individuals could be a spouse, a parent, a child, a sibling, a friend, or even a colleague. In such cases, our karmic mandate becomes to heal the equation. Moreover, the deeper our egoic feelings toward someone—especially attachment, anger, or aversion—the more there is to resolve, transform, and release. These emotions feed the ego and create difficult karmic debts. Attachment, in particular, is limiting because it leaves no room for space and freedom in relationships, leading to excessive emotional dependency, which can be damaging.

In a different context, when we have something unresolved with another soul, we may feel an intense urge to secure a place in their hearts. This may drive us to seek their approval or appreciation, which, in turn, pressures us to the point of exhaustion as we go out of our way to achieve it. And so, despite the inconvenience and stress, we end up doing more than we can handle. This compulsion arises from pending karma with that soul and often stems from low self-esteem—an ego-identified state that makes us feel inferior. In such cases, our pending karma is not only to resolve the equation with that soul but also to overcome our own weaknesses and transcend the ego. This is our unfinished business from past lives.

- **Scenario 5**

  In relationships, it is important to understand the difference between people we love naturally and people we struggle to love despite our best efforts. Those we love effortlessly are souls through whom we learnt to express love in past lives. So, our love for them flows naturally. But with certain individuals, no matter how much we try, love does not come easily. This is not due to a lack of effort or intention but because of unresolved past karma. These may be souls whose love we once failed to acknowledge or reciprocate. The imprint of that experience lingers in their subconscious, playing out as resistance from their end. Our pending karma in such relationships is to accept them despite their resistance—without expecting anything in return.

- **Scenario 6**

  If we experience strong feelings of aversion or rejection toward a family practice, belief system, superstition, way of life, or even the attitudes of our elders, this may indicate our pending karma. Sometimes, we may have been placed in such a family to break the continuity of something undesirable and introduce our loved ones to a new way of being. So, there will be a strong urge to change things, and we could be the turning point in our generational history, carrying the karmic responsibility to free future generations from unhealthy practices, traditions, or patterns.

Even if we remain unsuccessful in changing those who are too deeply identified with what we disapprove of, our role is to stop the cycle within ourselves. For at times, we are born into families not to change them but to ensure that something changes for the generations that follow. In such cases, we are the bridge to transformation. That is our pending karma.

- **Scenario 7**

In a difficult karmic relationship, it is not always others who are wrong and negative while we are the ones victimised. Sometimes, the pending karma is to recognise that the egoic patterns, tendencies, and behaviours we see in others are reflections of our own past actions and that we are meant to be the means of their healing. In some lifetime, we may have been the cause of their damage by interacting with these souls through an egoic personality. And so, those who traumatise us now could be the same souls we once hurt due to our ego in a previous exchange, creating negative karma. However, now that we have evolved in consciousness, the same flawed personality and behaviour that once belonged to us may seem problematic when mirrored in others.

But these souls are in an intimate relationship with us for a reason. They could be family, friends, or people with whom we spend a large part of our time so that we can help bring about the necessary change in them and heal the damage caused by our ignorant self. What is now unbearable in them may have been a part of our own personality in past lifetimes that we have forgotten. Our pending karma is to help these souls with patience, acceptance, compassion, guidance, and non-judgement.

- **Scenario 8**

  A heavy load of responsibilities that demand time, attention, effort, service, nourishment of others, or financial sustenance is often pending karma. It can be traced to a past where loved ones or people closely connected to us invested their time, effort, and money in us, only to be met with our ignorance, carelessness, or selfishness. And so, we created deeds with negative consequences. Now, as the fruit of that karma matures, it manifests as demanding responsibilities which are challenging and burdensome, yet necessary for our growth.

- **Scenario 9**

  Pending karma often manifests as boundaries or restrictions. There is only so much we can do about a karmic relationship or life situation. No matter how hard we try, we may feel confined or restrained. The areas of life where we feel the pinch of boundaries— or where setting boundaries is necessary for better mental health and peace—often have a karmic aspect attached.

Furthermore, restrictions could mean receiving less than expected or due whether in success, recognition, appreciation, love, care, acknowledgement, or even growth. These limitations indicate that our past influences the present in specific areas of life. The pending karma here is to move through life without complaint and to learn to appreciate the good in what is because we failed to do so in the past. This doesn't mean we should stop trying harder, but rather that we should do our best without attaching ourselves to a specific outcome.

- **Scenario 10**

When you do good for others, yet they remain thankless or fail to support you in your hour of need, it is likely that a past equation is influencing the results, or in other words, there is pending karma in such situations. Although such situations can lead to feelings of betrayal or disappointment, it is important to recognise that they are not intended to cause hurt or humiliation. Rather, they are meant to encourage you to cultivate humility and gratitude and to continue helping others without expectations.

That is because no one's behaviour is without reason, and life eventually returns everything. The very souls who fail to appreciate you now may be the ones whose help you overlooked in the past. A lack of gratitude in your own soul personality may be attracting such outcomes, and learning to cultivate appreciation is part of your pending karma.

- **Scenario 11**

Many of us may be tired of waiting for things to happen or things we have long wanted to see come to fruition. We may feel exhausted by an endless wait and perplexed as to why we are being tested for so long. But waiting for something we desperately want is part of a karmic agreement made with the self—an agreement where we choose to give our time in exchange for patience and inner strength, qualities our soul personality may lack.

When we operate through the tendency of desperation, we remain ego-driven. Desperation makes us weak and diminishes our prospects of attaining what we seek, as it creates the opposite energy of what is needed to attract it. It sends out the message that we are unwilling to be patient, unwilling to wait. It misaligns us with the present moment because desperation pulls us into the future rather than allowing us to be in the 'now'. It also breeds anxiety, stress, impatience, worry, fear, and restlessness—everything that is ego-identified.

Therefore, having to wait a long time for things to materialise in life indicates pending karma related to developing patience.

- **Scenario 12**

  Some of us feel that we haven't received what we deserve in life—things like respect, love, freedom, happiness, abundance, care, understanding, compassion, and success. Yet, at the most subtle level, these may be the very things we have long withheld from the world.

  So, when we blame the world for withholding certain things from us, our dear ones for not giving us enough attention, care, or love, or people at the workplace for denying us opportunities, growth, and success, we must understand that we are being denied what we have not yet learnt to give or share with others. Thus, in such scenarios, our pending karma is to cultivate the selfless act of giving all that is good and to reflect the spirit of generosity, which creates abundance in all areas of life.

- **Scenario 13**

  Going along life's usual road, if you ever stop and begin to ask questions, or if something catches your imagination and compels you to change direction, remember that your past has come calling! And no matter how hard you try to resist the change, you will be unable to stop yourself from making a transition. This is because pending karma often manifests as the need to change paths, take different routes, give up certain things, or embrace new risks even at the cost of stability and comfort. It arises in the form of an unfulfilled task, a desire, or a promise made to someone. Suddenly, it pushes us toward the unknown, the untraveled road, and compels us to do what no one expected of us.

- **Scenario 14**

  Regardless of how challenging your relationships are, if you are in them, if you continue to stay together, if you haven't yet stopped making the necessary effort or shown the courage to walk away, it is a pending karma that is holding you back. You would not be together otherwise. But this karma can only end through an approach that is non-judgemental and detached. If you respond with volatility and pain, or if you resent 'being together', you may be prolonging this for much longer. So, hang in there with courage and inner silence, trusting that you are in it for a peaceful closure. Remember, when peace is elusive and one continues to remain in the relationship, it may be because a major pending karma is destined for an amicable closure.

- **Scenario 15**

  Sometimes past connections may have been beautiful, but when a strong attachment existed in a close relationship, we return to be with the same souls again—this time, to dissolve those attachments and transform them into love. That is how we set each other free.

Attachment, being ego-identified, is unhealthy because it does not allow us to see ourselves as separate from the other. It creates no space, no freedom, and therefore, it is a weakness. Love, on the other hand, gives more depth and meaning to a relationship because, unlike attachment, it does not carry the baggage of expectations, fear, worry, or dependency. Love does not place pressure on the other person and allows individuality to flourish.

Thus, any relationship where we are overly attached to someone is likely to challenge us to reduce emotional dependency and rediscover our own individuality. In rare scenarios where attachment reflects a hardened ego, the pending karma may involve learning to live independently due to temporary separation or loss.

- **Scenario 16**

Pending karma is not just between two people; it also exists between individuals and the collective consciousness. This is because our state of being influences the collective. When we live happily and peacefully, we contribute to the strength of the collective consciousness. Likewise, when we are anxious, angry, fearful, or unhappy, we disturb the collective's peace and drain its energy.

Therefore, we must restore the positivity that was depleted from the collective. In other words, our pending karma is to contribute positively to life and the world at large. This may mean supporting causes that help the masses or contributing to the peace and well-being of others on a large scale. Most importantly, we must ensure that we remain aligned with our higher self and vibrate at the frequency of positive tendencies, which, in turn, energises the collective.

Additionally, if we have contributed to the collective's growth, peace, and power in the past, the same is returned to us manifold through the collective. At times, this comes in the form of mass support and popularity as a reward for good deeds. Our pending karma here is to receive such rewards with humility.

- **Scenario 17**

Finally, we all know that feeling when the heart says 'no', yet we still do something we never intended to. This is how karma works to extract its payback. There are times when we are caught between the head and the heart, unable to decide which way to go. We may want to choose what seems logical, yet somehow, we opt for the less desirable choice. Why does this happen? Because our pending karma beckons. There is something to settle in this direction, something long overdue. So, despite our doubt and hesitation, we relent.

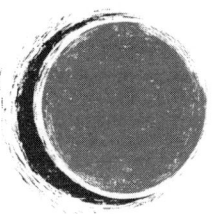

21

Working to End Karma

In the previous chapters, we discussed how the law of karma affects everyone without exception, and how both the good and the bad return with interest. Good pending karma is like a financial deposit, while negative karma is a debt, and both accumulate interest. The deposit is encashed upon maturity, and the debt is settled through instalments. That is how life returns everything; at some point, we get back what we have given. Understanding this truth is most important when working to end karma. Yet, when life brings us the negative consequences of our past deeds, the natural reaction is to ask, 'Why me?' However, there is no point in questioning the way life unfolds as it only wastes time and drains personal power.

So, what should our response be? Below are some key steps to help us effectively navigate the outcomes of our past actions.

- **Step 1: Don't Question**

The first and foremost step in addressing the consequences of our past actions is to recognise karma as past mistakes and avoid draining ourselves with negative thoughts and emotions. This means we need to embrace the way life orchestrates our experiences and resist reacting to challenges and situations in ways that push us toward ego-driven behaviour, which only further complicates what is already complex.

The key point to note is that with each major event in our lives, especially the unpleasant ones, if we have the wisdom to recognise how little we truly know and can respect the unfolding process, we will find peace. And this peace dissolves karma because, in its presence, negativity loses its momentum. Since peace comes from accepting things as they are, acceptance brings both freedom and power. Additionally, we need to realise that we receive what we have given, at some point in time. Understanding this truth is crucial when working to close karmic accounts. When we fail to understand this simple truth, we end up resisting karma, and in doing so, it only hits us harder. Therefore, we must face it with dignity, humility, maturity, and positivity. This approach makes the process easier and allows karmic chapters to close faster.

Facing karma correctly also means avoiding guilt over past mistakes. It is not about dwelling on what we may have done wrong but about recognising mistakes as opportunities for growth. Shifting into a learning mindset helps us gain deeper self-awareness, leading to meaningful positive change. Then comes the toughest and most crucial step: putting lessons into action. Whatever we realise at the level of thought must be reflected in our behaviour.

For example, if one recognises a pattern of anger—attracting angry people or situations that provoke aggression—the usual response might be to get triggered and escalate the conflict. But acting through one's lessons means choosing peace over anger. This is because the very tendencies that create karma will always be challenged when we face the consequences of past actions. If we remain aware of this, all we need to do is replace ego-driven tendencies with their opposite and resist the comfort of the ego. It comes with practice and by living with self-awareness. So, when anger arises, observe it but resist responding through it. It may surface as part of conditioned behaviour, which only changes with time, but what matters is not acting on it. Because only by refusing to engage in negative tendencies can we break old conditioning and free ourselves from habitual karmic patterns.

- **Step 2: Live Consciously**
To ascend to our higher self, which also means ending our karma, one must live consciously. This means:

1. Surrendering while doing one's best in any given situation.

2. Building good karma assets through good deeds.

3. Doing what is necessary for one's peace of mind and happiness and not remaining helpless in the face of karmic situations and experiences. Keeping the self free from guilt, hurt, damage, and stress. Because as we are, so is our energy, and so is our interaction with life. Therefore, when karma returns and we feel traumatised by any form of verbal, physical, psychological, or financial abuse, we must do whatever is necessary for our peace even if that means emotional and physical distancing in certain personal situations. Making peace a priority also means staying aligned with what is because peace is lost in imagining and reliving life situations that may not even be part of one's present reality. It is lost when we move away from what is to what could be or could have been. So, we must avoid such behaviour.

4. Doing what is right, not what is easy. Here, 'right' means stepping out of conditioned or habitual patterns of behaviour. It is never easy but always necessary, as facing karma with patience and resilience fosters growth and evolution, which means we face milder

situations where experiences and people don't destroy our self-esteem and aren't harmful or emotionally damaging. While they may not meet our expectations—because karma has a role to play—there is still scope for adjustments, understanding, and reconciliation. In such cases, where stepping away may seem like the easier option, staying becomes necessary to resolve the karma and to live through one's higher self.

5. Being aware of right and wrong and choosing what feels right despite the challenges. Right and wrong must be evaluated in the context of what serves our higher self.

6. Staying true to one's conscience and doing what eliminates confusion, doubt, regret, overanalysis, and overthinking. These arise when we draw unnecessary assumptions and listen too much to the mind's chatter while ignoring intuition. Therefore, we must avoid obsessing over the 'why' behind everything or discussing things beyond our control.

- **Step 3: Put a Stop to Ego-Driven Behaviour**
  The third and final step is to identify egoistic patterns through greater self-awareness. This will help you stop ego-driven behaviour. If you or someone you know

struggles with ego, simply observe the behaviour as a witness without attaching emotions to it, identifying with it, or judging it. Do not energise such behaviour by investing your thoughts or emotions in it. Instead, learn to watch and silence the mental commentary prompted by the ego. This allows you to focus on settling karma.

As discussed earlier, stepping out of ego means doing the exact opposite of what your ego-driven mind wants. This means facing your fears, since fear is the ego's favourite tool. We are here to release fear, not carry it from one lifetime to another. Otherwise, the ego persists, and karma only becomes more intimidating.

In a nutshell, to break free from fear, we must stop investing in it. The best way to do so is through less thought and more action as it opposes fear. This means:

1. If we are afraid to speak up, we must say what needs to be said the moment fear urges us to stay silent.

2. If we are afraid to take risks, we must take them more often.

3. If we fear losing something or someone, we must live in the present instead of an imagined future. Fully experiencing people and things in the moment, rather than disconnecting due

to an imagined future, helps release fear and dissolve attachment.

Overall, to overcome fear, we must invest in positivity in various ways. What we read, watch, listen to, talk about, or discuss must be positive. A positive mindset aligns us with a higher frequency and leaves no room for negative behaviour, which is imperative to ending karma.

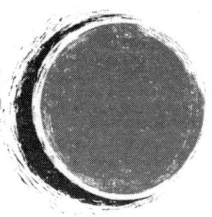

22

Relationship Karma

What Is Relationship Karma?

In simple terms, relationship karma refers to the heavy emotions of a past energy exchange that remain with a soul in its subconscious recordings. These recordings create vibrations that prompt individuals to behave in certain ways—actions and reactions that may at times seem entirely unjustified because their origins lie in a past that could be vastly different from the present. This is why people can feel uncomfortable with each other for no apparent reason, and relationships can become complicated without any serious fault. In other words, differences may arise due to past karmic connections that remain unknown to those involved.

Relationships are born out of karmic connections from past lives. They carry the majority of our debts and balances, which is why they need to be handled with care despite their complexities. The truth is that we do not meet anyone by chance; every present-day encounter is deeply tied to the past. We meet those with whom our karma has ripened, and the fruit is ready to be served—bitter, sour, sweet, or tasteless—our experience of this fruit depends on the seed that was sown in previous lifetimes. We meet certain souls again to settle karma and heal broken hearts. We cross paths to learn from each other and free one another from negative emotions accumulated in past lives. As discussed, these emotions persist as vibrations, creating discomfort between two people, even when their current identities or relationships differ from before. The higher purpose of relationship karma is to erase heavy soul recordings that cause mutual discomfort. Thus, we must take our relationships seriously and always put our best foot forward in every connection we form. We should try to make them work, and if they fail, we must give them a dignified closure.

What is important to note here is that the people we are surrounded by, we have known them before. There has been an exchange of energy and shared experiences with all of them. They continue to be in our lives because there is still something to share or something to strengthen in each other. We exist within families and relationships to resolve the past while fostering growth and maturity in the present.

So, it can be anyone—a parent, sibling, child, friend, partner, spouse, colleague, or relative—who pushes us toward growth and maturity by challenging us mentally and emotionally. But we must handle them with intelligence and care, as they offer us the opportunity to grow and evolve as beings. They may be hard to please, but if we can accept them, adjust, accommodate, be flexible and compassionate, or simply maintain our composure and dignity in the relationship, we will be able to grow as individuals and resolve past mistakes. This is because the energy of such mistakes remains as karma even as people change their physical forms. Additionally, what we do not resolve now is carried forward to another life, where we meet the same set of souls with whom we need to make peace. And when we meet again, the complexities of the present catch us unaware, making us question everything in the relationship. And the more times we have met certain souls across lifetimes, the greater and tougher the karmic mandate may be to adjust, accept, and harmonise with them. Therefore, the key is to honour all relationships as soul connections and to see the people in our lives as past energy exchanges. They have returned either to give what they owed us or to take back what we owed them.

It is also important to remember that in relationships, our soul is drawn to frequencies and vibrations that may either be similar to ours or radically different. We choose those souls as a family from whom we can learn about ourselves—souls who can trigger transformation within us. Or we choose those whom we can help change and grow. And as souls, we are all equal and are simply arranged in relationships where the maximum debts of karma can be settled, where love and freedom can replace attachment and fear. Yet, we are conditioned to see relationships through labels, which create expectations, beliefs, hierarchies, and rigid approaches to how we interact with others and how they should respond to us.

If only we could understand our journey as souls together, if only we altered our consciousness to see everyone close to us as equals, we would not accumulate karmic debts, which arise from negative emotions and interactions rooted in failed expectations and conditioned ways of viewing relationships through labels. These labels create rigid concepts of relationships, preventing deeper connections. We measure relationships against these concepts, and when they fall short, we feel disappointed. And this is how karma starts accumulating. Thus, we must stop viewing people through the lens of relationship labels and concepts and recognise that we are journeying with souls who have been with us for lifetimes. The less we define people through labels, the deeper our connection becomes at the soul level, until all that remains is love or the ego dissolves, expectations fall away, and we become free.

The vital thing to note here is that it is only our conceptual understanding of relationships that disrupts harmony and creates conflict. Because concepts define relationships in a certain way, they lead to expectations, comparisons, grudges, and rifts. And so, if you have a difficult equation with your parents, sibling, friend, or spouse, you must break this chain of negativity right here. Or if you are a parent and your child is difficult, you must not let that define your relationship. After all, you are together because your karmas are deeply intertwined. You may have reversed roles, but you have been together in previous lifetimes as close relatives or associates. Remember, you are now in this relationship because you need to set each other free. The way to do this is by giving your best to the relationship without expecting the other person to be the way you want them to be. This means that you need to relate to each other as souls rather than through the labels of your relationship. It also requires understanding that as souls, we are all at different stages of progress, maturity, and growth, which may not necessarily align with our physical age or the human roles we play in a family. This awareness helps us accept people without judgement and heal past karmic accounts much faster. It also enables us to handle relationships with greater maturity and aids our own growth, which is the higher purpose of karma.

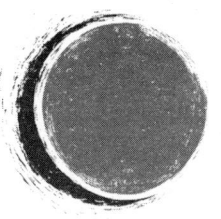

23

Ending Relationship Karma

In the previous chapters, we discussed how relationships are not only a test of our character but also a mirror that reveals it. They offer valuable opportunities for the evolution of our consciousness and personal growth. As such, relationships must be approached in ways that enhance our awareness and understanding. But how do we achieve this? Relationship karma can push us to extremes, challenging us in ways we never anticipated. So, how can we navigate relationships to minimise karmic repercussions? How can we grow while managing relationships that challenge our emotions and test our patience?

Here are a few ways that can be useful:

1. Take the Initiative to Heal the Equation

It is important to understand that people aren't inherently difficult, nor do they choose to be the way they are; they simply haven't known another way. They engage with the world through a consciousness that is burdened by past experiences and is devoid of joy and goodness. And if you find yourself at the receiving end of their inner turmoil, understand that this is the result of the past—one that you may not be aware of.

For instance, a difficult parent-child relationship is often the result of generations of karmic entanglement waiting to be resolved. It is complicated because these may be the same souls from the same lineage, repeating mistakes, mistrust, and misgivings across lifetimes. This creates generational karma that needs resolution. In fact, all turbulent family equations are often a cluster of unhealed souls feeding off each other. In other words, our family comprises souls we haven't just met before; rather, based on past interactions, we have chosen these very souls for our spiritual evolution and growth. This evolution happens naturally through karmic settlement, by learning to change for the better, and by living with people who challenge us to think differently— people with whom we must live through our higher self, which is inherently more kind, loving, caring, forgiving, accepting, flexible, and brave.

And the toughest karmic equation that cannot be left unresolved is the one between a parent and child. This is a karma one must face until it runs its course. The nature of the relationship is such that one cannot simply walk away or exit prematurely. Our parents are souls on a long journey with us, and our shared history involves deep emotional give-and-take. This equation needs healing, not complaints. Here, it is vital to recognise that our parents may have been our children, siblings, or friends in past lives. They could have been anyone known to us. This connection has only grown stronger because the karmic knots between us have tightened. What they owed us, they honoured by bringing us into this world and raising us. What we owe them, we must honour by being there for them regardless of how things have been. That is how the knots loosen, and both become free.

That said, parenting can go wrong—sometimes terribly wrong. This happens because the soul connection is karmic. Parents and children share a long, forgotten history, and as souls on an extended journey together, they have reinforced their karmic knots by resisting change, clinging to conditioning, and acting from ego. Complications arise due to excessive emotional dependency, attachment, or unresolved give-and-take that has accumulated over time. This applies to all close relationships where past energy exchanges have been heavy and dark, making the present equation difficult. However, wasting time on analysis, hurt, or blame serves no purpose. What matters is that someone must heal the equation.

So, between two people, the one who drops the ego achieves freedom. In fact, they also set the other free. They break negative patterns, raise their frequency, and create positivity. And if doing something positive feels too difficult, at the very least, one must stop feeding into the emotional chaos. One must also allow the other—who may not be ready for change—to operate from their current state of consciousness while seeing the situation without labels, judgement, or absorption of its negativity. This alone breaks the karmic momentum and moves the relationship toward healing.

2. Alter Your Response

What is even more damaging than difficult karma is holding onto the negative emotions and feelings associated with it. When you hold on to hurt, the equation becomes even more karmic. So, let it go. Don't feed it with your feelings and emotions. You have already done that in the negative past you shared with the one with whom there is suffering in the present. The karmic story continues because the response being given is negative. If there were no past deeds with serious consequences, or if there had been no karmic interaction before, the response from both sides wouldn't be so emotional or complicated. Therefore, a better interaction—through a better response—needs to be created for feelings on both sides to become lighter. This is an essential part of ending karma.

Ending karma, however, does not mean passively accepting wrongdoing. It simply means that in each situation, we do what needs to be done, but without creating hate, anger, bitterness, revulsion, or a desire for revenge. Such emotions are self-destructive and only deepen karmic bondage. Thus, the more emotionally stable we are, the faster we burn our karma and heal past accounts. So, there will be people who will trigger our negative reactions causing discomfort and tempting us to respond in kind.

But reacting negatively doesn't just create more negativity, one also absorbs the negativity of the other person and the situation, further deepening karmic complications by lowering our own consciousness. So, when you are good to people and they do not reciprocate, set them free. Release them from the prison of your mind. Understand that your story with them was never about receiving positivity in return; rather, it was about learning to accept those you may have disappointed before. After all, we don't go anywhere. Our karmic knots pull us back into the lives of the same souls to whom we owe a payback. Additionally, if you continue thinking or feeling negatively about someone, those very thoughts will manifest as anger from both sides, making the equation even more karmic. And if this karma isn't resolved now, it will only become harder the next time you meet.

So, try staying neutral or non-reactive, or, if possible, start thinking positively about the other person. Be sure that one day, those thoughts will manifest as peace and acceptance from both sides.

3. Don't Extend the Suffering

The less emotional your response to your karmic troubles, the less miserable, sad, burdened, hopeless, and victimised you will feel. So, all you need to do is stop thinking emotionally about your troubles. This entails:

- Not empowering the situation by giving it your thought energy.
- Not connecting too deeply.
- Saying little and thinking nothing about the people linked to you through relationship karma.
- Avoiding discussing your problems with others, as this only strengthens them and extends both suffering and karma, unless you are seeking professional help.

By following these steps, you prevent unnecessary suffering and allow karma to dissolve more quickly because karma extends itself through continuous suffering.

Here, it is also important to note that our suffering must end with the karmic experience itself, rather than continuing in our thoughts, feelings, and emotions long after. This means that when karma operates through people who reject us, deny us what we deserve, betray, or overlook us, we need not carry the weight of their actions as our own. Instead, we must unlock the gates that confine us both and set each other free. However, in such situations, our instinct is to create emotional hurt and suffering. What we fail to understand is that we are locked in a karmic situation, and no matter how terribly someone behaves, we must stop hurting ourselves because of their actions. It is a bitter account from the past that has created these life scenarios. There is already a great deal of negative energy in the equation. But when we respond with negatively charged emotions, we feed the karma, allowing it to grow, and we continue suffering in our journey with such souls.

Thus, the end of karma comes when we stop nourishing it—when we pull back. So, even when our mind urges us to suffer and complain, we must refrain. The end of karma begins by withholding any further energy from what is already negative.

4. Operate with Honesty

Honesty is a powerful tendency that connects us with our higher self. It is essential for transforming our equations from negative to positive and for ending the play of ego. Since most relationships crumble due to ego, honesty helps create real, meaningful, and lasting connections. Where there is honesty, there is no ego, primarily because there is no fear. And where there is no fear, a pure and powerful vibration exists, making relationships effortless.

Honesty also fosters love and appreciation. An honest person has no hidden agendas, no pretence. They have nothing to hide, leaving no room for doubt or insecurity. This makes those around them feel light and energised, helping to create karma-free relationships.

At times, however, honesty may backfire, particularly when karmic roots are strong, and the other person is more reactive than understanding. In such situations, honesty must be expressed with tact. Speech and expression should be polite and sensitive, ensuring the other person is not offended. When honesty is conveyed with inner stability and dignity, the energy reaching the reactive person is bound to have a calming effect. Thus, it is not just honesty but also the way it is communicated that helps diffuse tension, build acceptance, and break the rigid nature of karma that binds two people.

5. Replace Expectations with Acceptance

When you don't accept people as they are and expect them to be as you want them to be, it builds relationship karma. This suffocates the other person or creates unrest in them, leading to turbulence in relationships. Often, it is our expectations and mental conditioning that make us believe people should act a certain way—that they must be kind, must return our goodness, love, and generosity, or reciprocate our willingness to adjust or do things for them. We believe that when people don't respond as we expect, they are mean, selfish, or unfair. But through the lens of karma, we can never truly say what is fair or unfair.

The truth is that karma operates beyond our awareness, orchestrating specific experiences with certain people to settle unresolved accounts. Everything happens for a reason, governed by the ever-active law of cause and effect. This is why acceptance is the highest spiritual practice. It not only leads to inner peace but also breaks the karmic cycle, which prolongs itself through resistance to what is. So, while it is natural to expect kindness or support from others—especially in times of need—when something expected is denied, avoid becoming bitter. Perhaps, in that denial, you are being saved from another debt. Perhaps, the denial is the way a karmic chapter is meant to close. Perhaps, what was denied was your payback.

Remember, the key to dissolving karma lies in responding wisely to difficult people and situations. While we all expect to be treated fairly and with dignity, this may not always be the case in karmic relationships. What we expect, we may not receive. However, it is high-frequency behaviour that ultimately helps. So, if we can accept others as they are and treat them as we wish to be treated, we take a significant step toward dissolving karma. Acceptance eases tension and creates a positive vibe. When we accept others without judgement or criticism, we calm their energy and make them less reactive. This also steers them toward a more positive thought process, which may be more challenging in relationships where karmic payback is involved. A difficult relationship, which might otherwise be overwhelming, becomes easier to navigate through acceptance. It also prevents further karmic entanglement, which is essential for resolving karma.

6. Don't Play the Blame Game

Our negative accounts naturally create situations where we resort to blaming others for their misdeeds or behaviour that may not be acceptable to us. But what we forget is that relationships are karmic accounts, and an account means there has been an energy exchange in the past. So, there is continuity, and in negative accounts, the continuity is of negativity. This creates more room for the blame game, and often, an entire life passes by in claiming one's innocence and blaming the other.

In reality, however, no one is to be blamed. Karma has its threads in our unknown past, and the pattern that these threads weave in the present moment traces back to that past. We go through life unaware, unconscious, and unfamiliar with the real cause of our difficulties. We resist what is, feeling distressed, anxious, and victimised, but little do we understand that what is happening now is simply a result of our past.

Additionally, blame often continues through abuse, which manifests in two ways. One is the actual event, and the other is our mental construct of it—the way we repeatedly relive it. The latter is more damaging, as it cements our conditioning as a permanent victim. This victim identity grows stronger with the constant recollection of past unpleasant memories, fuelled by emotional reactions. But this identity is an illusion, not the truth. It is merely an overactive ego that expands when we cling to a false image of the self. To break free from this victim identity, we must make a conscious effort to stop reliving the past. Only when we stop feeding painful memories with our thoughts and emotions do we stop seeing ourselves as victims. And that is where blame ends.

In summary, blame only reinforces karma. Letting go of blame in difficult relationships is the first step toward dissolving it. And for those who understand this, there is peace, and past accounts can be healed.

7. Give but Don't Count

When you stop keeping a balance sheet of give and take in relationships, that is when your debt releases you. But the more you calculate this exchange, the tighter karma's grip becomes. Because if a relationship is conditional—based on give and take (whether emotional, physical, or material)—then it is not a relationship; it is a transaction between two egos. And this transaction only tightens karmic knots.

The truth is you don't truly give anything to anyone. What you give is what you owe, and it traces back to a past you don't remember. So, it is pointless to be arrogant about what you give to someone or resentful about what you don't receive in return. The help you offer, the times you rescue someone in need, or any act of generosity may simply be a major karmic payback. However, when you take credit for it or expect something in return, you settle nothing. This is because what you give is linked to a past energy exchange with that same person, and thus, it is important to give because this energy needs to be transformed.

Therefore, the more humble you are about what you give or do for someone, the faster your karmic debts resolve. It is the act of selfless giving—without expectation—that not only cleanses our aura but also erases the darker recordings of karma from our soul.

8. Invest Time

Time plays a major role in ending karma. When you give time and attention to someone, you also heal your past accounts with them. Giving time and attention means making that person feel important, respected, and cared for. It creates positivity in a relationship. And regardless of how challenging this relationship may be due to past karma, when someone can feel your wholehearted presence during the time you spend together, it allows good energy to enter the equation.

Furthermore, your undivided attention can help you harmonise with that person in ways that create good vibes between you. It makes them feel valued, and what better way to heal past accounts than this? A simple act of being present with someone, listening to them with full attention, is also a way to heal them—provided you don't judge them in any way and remain present without mental noise. In today's world, where giving undivided attention to our loved ones is increasingly difficult, understanding the connection between time and karma becomes even more crucial.

9. Honour Your Duty and Responsibilities

A major cause of negative karma in relationships is a past where responsibilities were not honoured and duties towards loved ones remained unfulfilled. When people are ignored, abandoned, or taken for granted despite their efforts for us, it creates significant karmic debts. Likewise, when a close relation is dependent on us, and we neglect their needs or fail to care for them, especially when they completely rely on us, karmic debts arise. This is because the duties and responsibilities one has in relationships already indicate a strong karmic connection from the past. When we ignore these responsibilities and fail to play our part, karmic accounts deepen and eventually return as burdens we cannot escape.

A good way to resolve relationship karma is by honouring your responsibilities in life. Failing to fulfil our obligations in relationships creates a heavier burden that can become a hindrance to the life we wish to build. And there are people who are unable to pursue their dreams or live the life of their choice due to overwhelming family responsibilities. This is a karmic block, stemming from past neglect of duty. Such individuals have likely been selfish or careless in their past. Their present responsibilities, however, offer them an opportunity to change these tendencies and elevate their character.

10. Leave, If It Saves Your Peace

Often, we cling to unhappy relationships or life situations simply for the sake of carrying on. We hold on, hoping that things will improve. We believe that, someday, everything will change, and peace will be restored. And so, we go on and on . . . for years, even a lifetime. But in doing so, we often remain peaceless and resist accepting things as they are, draining ourselves in the process.

The truth is that everything good arises from a place of peace. So, when faced with a difficult situation or relationship, don't waste too much energy trying to fight reality. Just understand that there is a complicated past to it, and that is why you can't have it any other way. Put simply, live it, accept it, be dignified with it but don't add more negativity or sorrow to it. If you must, move away gracefully. Don't let it beat you down or make you feel like a victim. And certainly, don't allow yourself to remain in pain, misery, anger, or strife as karma only compounds this way.

If you choose to distance yourself from people or situations that disrupt your inner state, ensure they no longer occupy your thoughts and emotions—especially in a negative way. Holding onto negative feelings keeps the karmic equation active. Therefore, let every parting, of any kind, be peaceful. Otherwise, be sure to meet the same person in another form, in another life, and amid greater chaos. And if nothing works out and you must leave a relationship, part with empathy, compassion, and forgiveness. This lightens the karma. But at no cost should you carry hurt, anger, or revenge in your mind as these translate into major karmic debts.

Moreover, do not stay in abusive or deeply unhappy relationships. They will leave you incapable of creating healthy relationships anywhere. If a relationship doesn't work out despite genuine effort, rather than continuing to struggle, stay apart. More ·importantly, maintain a peaceful energy toward the same person.

There is no doubt that unhappy relationships serve karmic lessons, and they demand immense patience and fortitude. But remember, this must not come at the cost of your peace and sanity. Sometimes, karma is resolved better by leaving and creating a better life for yourself. It is resolved by living in peace and radiating peace, not through restless compromises or blind hope for change.

11. Learn to Move On

If someone doesn't want you in their life—whether it is a friend, a partner, or even a close family member—do not force yourself upon them by trying to please them or by expecting them to be kind to you. Sometimes, karmic settlement comes in the form of rejection, and all one needs to do is accept it and move on with dignity. Also, don't expect people—or yourself—to remain the same always. As we settle our karmic debts, we are meant to move on.

The key to relationships is understanding that people change. One must not stay attached to the past image of a person. This helps in dropping expectations or judgements connected to that person and ensures that the equation remains light and karma-free. At the same time, don't live in denial. Accept that when relationships run their course, they end regardless of how or why. What matters is that you set yourself and the other person free.

It is crucial to realise that moving on is necessary. No matter how easy or difficult it seems, it is part of our karmic settlement. It is also a healthier way to live. Moving on is a process we owe to life, for only when we close one chapter can we open new ones. And in doing so, we allow ourselves to explore the unexpected, encounter the unplanned, and discover— whether for better or worse—the possibilities that lie ahead. We grow, we evolve, and through it all, we deepen in learning and maturity.

12. Don't Insist on Changing People

Attachment in relationships comes from the ego. Attachment isn't love, and so, when we are attached, we tend to see the other person through an image we have created in our mind. And when they don't fit into that image, we try to impose change. We feel the need to see this change happen because attachment, unlike love, isn't freedom; it is control. And control complicates relationships.

We must understand that people cannot change until they are ready. There are three primary reasons for this:

a) People don't change because they haven't completed their set of karmic paybacks in this life. Until they do, they won't gain the necessary learning, which is essential for change.

b) People don't change because they are souls, and souls carry a past unique to them— an accumulation of lifetimes filled with experiences that have shaped their present state of being. This past can only be overcome in a specific way and at a specific time. Until then, they cannot be forced into change. Depending on their individual capacity, it will take them time to alter their conditioning and embrace a new way of being.

c) People don't change because the people we expect to change are in a karmic transaction with us. They won't change until they have influenced us to develop patience, compassion, acceptance, forgiveness, and unconditional love. They are in our lives for a reason. And until we change for the better, neither the karmic account ends, nor can we expect the other person to change.

13. Have a Compassionate Approach

Compassion means that we understand and accept that we don't know the larger purpose of anything and that a higher law governs all of us, and we must respect it. It means that we don't know why people are the way they are or why they lead a certain kind of life. It means that we accept that we are not the creators of human journeys, nor are we in a position to decide how others should or should not be. Because of this, we must never judge anyone. Not only is judgement bad karma, but when we judge something or someone, we create strong emotions, and these emotions lead to thought patterns that intensely connect us to another's life. And it is the same life we eventually attract, as we remain consumed by such people's character.

Compassion means accepting others as they are and understanding that they are conditioned to think and behave in a certain way. Until they reach a point in their journey where they grow tired of their conditioning, transformation may not be possible for them. Compassion is important because when we judge others, we make them uncomfortable and anxious. Our energy makes them feel threatened, turning the interaction karmic. However, when we incorporate genuine appreciation and patience into our compassionate behaviour, we contribute positively to a negative situation. Appreciation is empowering and helps people feel comfortable with us, leaving no room for negativity. Patience, in turn, gives the other person space as it allows the relationship to breathe.

Overall, compassion is the bridge that takes us to the finish line of karmic settlement and helps us enjoy the rewards of spiritual growth, as having compassion for people and refraining from judgement disentangles karmic knots faster.

14. Show Accountability

The ability to own up to mistakes and take accountability dissolves major karmic burdens attached to both the mistake and the relationship. But the ego resists accepting mistakes—it loves to defend itself. Yet, in any equation, when we recognise where we may have gone wrong and accept our mistake, the ego takes a fall. And when we overcome the ego, the karma attached to the mistake dissolves.

Mistakes in our life are an opportunity to check the ego and make amends by evaluating the situation honestly and truthfully through a new consciousness. But when we allow the ego to get the better of us, the negative karma attached to the mistake solidifies and returns to us. However, when we show accountability and acknowledge where we may have faltered— when we genuinely feel apologetic—we demonstrate humility, which is the opposite of the ego. Humility helps dissolve karma because it raises our frequency and aligns us with our higher self. It allows us to rise above the negativity of the mistake and the impending karma. That said, it is important to remember that offering an apology does not mean carrying guilt. One must be cautious because guilt is a negative emotion and can extend karma rather than resolve it.

15. Forgive

Forgiveness means accepting someone as they are. Forgiveness doesn't mean you continue getting emotionally consumed by someone. It means you stop bringing your shared past into the present and save yourself from succumbing to mindless thinking or any kind of emotional manipulation that could pull you into a pool of negativity. It also means applying emotions only to the positive aspects of the relationship so that you keep creating the right energy for transformation.

To put it simply, forgiveness means you understand:

- That people didn't give you what they didn't have.
- They didn't give you what they didn't understand.
- They didn't give you what was denied to them.

And so, it is you who must break their negativity because such people aren't self-aware. They are ignorant and lost, trapped in their menacing egos, manifesting as insecurity, fear, low self-esteem, and anger. Such people carry a heavy soul recording, and they could be anyone—a parent, spouse, sibling, friend, or even a colleague with whom your relationship is complicated. But since they are in your life, rather than leaving things as they are, you need to make the relationship more cordial. Otherwise, the negativity of karma may create prolonged unpleasantness and prevent you from closing the karmic account. So, you must approach the relationship with deeper intelligence. And since settling a karmic debt means to give something positive to end what is negative, forgiveness is pure positivity.

16. Take Care of Yourself

As the negative consequences of your past deeds return, people may cheat you, deceive you, hurt you, give up on you, or leave you. However, what you do to yourself is far more important and relevant than what anyone else does. By reliving moments of hurt, deception, pain, manipulation, abuse, exploitation, or even failure—by carrying them as baggage—you rob yourself of dignity, devalue your life, lower your self-esteem, disturb your peace, and make your scars permanent. And there cannot be anything more karmic than this. It inflates your ego and exposes you to the dangers of negative behaviour, which is the root cause of karma creation.

Remember, in life, you can do what is right only when you continue feeling right. Wrong feelings don't lead to the right actions or results. So, while facing our karmic debts, our inner state is most important. And since the nature of karma is to challenge us and destabilise our inner balance, stopping our response to emotional triggers allows us to address things correctly.

Therefore, in any karmic situation, our attention should be on the self. This involves:

a) How are we responding, feeling, thinking, and understanding?

b) What are we really creating within?

c) What are we absorbing?

If the external situation is disturbing our inner state, then everything is only becoming more intense and complicated. Hence, we must do whatever it takes to prevent more negativity from taking over. And this is only possible when we remain attentive to ourselves and learn to shift our thoughts and feelings to a more neutral or positive state.

Further, a few things can help you preserve your peace and positivity in relationships. These relate to your approach and behaviour, such as:

a) Don't make a relationship the centre of your universe. Don't always think or talk about it. Too much energy directed toward any relationship can suffocate it. Divide your time and attention with greater care.

b) Expect little or nothing in return, but don't tolerate abuse or manipulation. Be dignified when dealing with the latter and convey your protest clearly.

c) Engage in the relationship with greater self-awareness. Pay attention to your state of mind when you are with the other person. Make sure there is inner balance.

d) Give only as much as your inner capacity permits. Don't overdo the giving or the niceness. Understand your threshold and respect it. Often, we give or do far more than our inner capacity allows—more than what feels comfortable—and that is where we falter. Anything that exceeds our own capacity becomes artificial and forced, complicating the equation. So, be nice, but also ensure that you feel nice, as any kind of forced behaviour creates anxiety and restlessness and disrupts peace in the equation. It is precisely in such moments that the other person may not appreciate your niceness or effort, as your energy will convey the underlying confusion.

It is important to recognise that when you face a karmic situation, the spotlight is on you. And if you can maintain inner stability, if you can stop yourself from getting emotionally worked up, if you can preserve your peace and positivity for your own sake, karma ends.

So, do your best in your relationships, but let your inner peace guide you. Don't cross the line that takes you from peace to a negative emotion. Remember, in relationships, what matters more is the inner feeling, not just the outward doing.

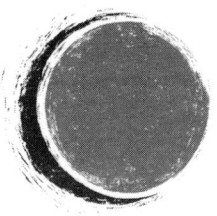

24

Money Karma

We build karma with both people and things, including wealth and money. The energy we invest in generating income or making expenditures creates a response that mirrors our own energy. If the energy we invest is flawed, the response is also flawed. Since energy is subtle, it is influenced by our soul recordings, i.e., past patterns shape the present. So, when our efforts to make money don't yield the desired results or when we encounter unnecessary expenses and losses, it is our own energy that attracts these experiences. This experience reflects karma.

The truth is, we can never get away with making money or any sort of gains the wrong way. Even if we believe human laws can be broken, nothing escapes the law of karma. The law of the land may fail—a lawbreaker, a criminal, or a culprit may be let off due to lack of evidence— but the law of karma always takes its course, delivering punishment to the guilty in some form or another. It may take time for karma to yield the consequences of one's deeds, and sometimes the punishment may come a few or even several lifetimes later, but a recorded offence is never spared its due reckoning.

This can be understood through real-life examples, where we see:

- Innocent people getting punished or penalised for an offence they did not commit in their present life.
- People being wrongly framed and spending time in prison for no fault of their own.
- Small financial frauds or mistakes leading to severe consequences.
- People facing heavy financial losses due to unforeseen misfortunes.
- People struggling to earn the right way in their chosen field of work.
- People losing their health, with money getting drained in expensive treatments.
- People unable to generate savings despite their best efforts.

Therefore, what may seem unfair or unexpected in the present is often karma returning with lessons for past mistakes. 'Past' here refers to past lives. As the consequences of one's past offences mature, people face unexpected difficulties in their present life—ones they may not seem guilty of or deserving of. Yet, they must undergo these experiences to learn and evolve from the deeds they committed in the past.

A question to consider here is what gives rise to money karma? The answer is that it results from using the wrong tendencies while creating wealth. And money karma returns to bite when those tendencies persist, forcing deeper lessons in financial matters. So, if someone accumulated wealth through greed in a past life, they may now struggle to make money despite their best efforts, without understanding why. The lingering greed and desire for more may push them to work harder, but the results may remain unrewarding.

While this may feel like punishment, until they stop using greed or excessive desire as their primary motivation for work, they will not achieve the right results. They may still work hard and pursue their goals with great intensity, but their intention must be pure. The driving force behind their actions must be sincerity or love for their work, not the desire for massive gains. Remember, karma demands the necessary replacement of what is unhealthy in one's soul personality. As long as low-frequency tendencies driven by the ego persist, they will not receive the compensation or gains they believe they deserve.

Ego in money karma manifests as tendencies like attachment, greed, lust for possessions, arrogance, and self-centeredness—tendencies that the karmic law seeks to counter. Such tendencies may reflect in habitual patterns or behaviours continuing from one's past, such as:

1. Making someone else settle one's bills when one is capable of or required to pay them.
2. Not paying one's staff their salaries on time.
3. Not giving people what they deserve for their efforts or withholding their fair share.
4. Stealing money.
5. Being stingy and avoiding spending due to fear or attachment to money.
6. Overindulgence and wasteful spending.
7. Overcharging.

Or one may commit major financial offences such as:

1. Making money through unethical means.
2. Tax evasion.
3. Intentionally defaulting on financial debts or bank loans.
4. Hoarding unaccounted wealth.
5. Engaging in corruption.
6. Committing financial fraud.
7. Duping people for financial gains.
8. Exploiting the underprivileged.

All such actions amount to monetary abuse and have consequences. In more severe cases, the karmic penalty may be heavier, depending on the nature of one's deeds and the time taken for their repercussions to surface.

When karmic consequences related to money arise, one's prosperity may remain blocked, or even if they are prosperous, their wealth may be lost in unexpected and undesirable ways. This occurs because they have abused money in some form, whether in their present or past lifetimes. It indicates that the qualities of fairness, honesty, selflessness, kindness, generosity, lawfulness, and ethical conduct in financial matters remain underdeveloped in their character. As a result, they may face challenges related to money and encounter various consequences to recognise their own inner deficiencies.

Understanding money-related karma is essential because money is a significant aspect of life. When wealth is hoarded through unfair means, when taxes are evaded, and when dealings are unscrupulous, a painful destiny is created—not just for oneself but also for future generations. This is because wealth is consumed by both the present and future generations, and the energy attached to such money carries forward. The energy of ill-gotten wealth aligns with negativity, manifesting as disease, disputes, mishaps, depression, and other hardships. Gradually, these negative influences take root in our homes and lives. Monetary abuse, therefore, attracts difficulties for both the individual and their family, creating a complicated karmic trap that affects generations to come.

Thus, it is crucial to approach financial matters with fairness and respect for money. Transforming our attitude toward money helps resolve money-related karma and invites opportunities for lasting prosperity.

The following are good money habits that help invoke the energy of prosperity and dissolve any karmic debts attached to wealth:

1. Keep Circulating Money

Don't be a hoarder or a miser. If you are, you give stagnant energy to your money, preventing it from growing. It also indicates that you are undeserving because you aren't capable of sharing your wealth. However, when you spend money for the right reasons and keep it circulating, the energy of money remains active and charged, attracting better wealth prospects because that same money returns to you with interest.

Spending money for the right reasons also brings more positivity to your own energy, as you begin operating with detachment, wisdom, and fearlessness. And when you spend money with the right energy, you purify it.

2. Do Not Abuse Money

Spend prudently, not compulsively. Don't waste money on things that aren't necessary. Do not overspend or indulge in excessive luxury just to boost your ego because ego thrives on display. The bigger the ego, the greater the need to showcase power and wealth for unnecessary reasons.

Often, you may see someone wealthy who enjoys extravagant spending on luxury, celebrations, or events, and assume that things are going well for them. What you don't realise is how their own wealth may be turning against them because their relationship with money is not positive.

Extravagance is not a healthy interaction with wealth. Spending obscene amounts purely for ego gratification is an abuse of wealth. And not even the affluent are entitled to misuse their money this way, let alone those who go beyond their means to spend on social events, celebrations, or personal upgrades. So, if you see someone spending recklessly on luxury goods, parties, eating out, shopping, or vacations, understand that their wealth is working against them. Always remember that wealth attains dignity through balance—a balance between charity and self-indulgence. Otherwise, it becomes a karmic burden.

Some other ways of creating a problematic equation with wealth include competing in or comparing matters of material possessions, not paying dues on time, defaulting on payments, evading taxes, or building an extravagant life through multiple debts. All these qualify as abuse and lead to karmic bondage.

3. Show Generosity

Money karma becomes a source of problems in one's life when one measures every bit of what they give. So, when you serve or work for someone in exchange for money, make sure you do a little more than what's required and fully satisfy that person. Similarly, when you are paying someone for a service, offering a little extra as an incentive for work well done is always good karma.

People with money karma often show a tendency to take things for free. But this habit also implies that they should be prepared to receive less for their own efforts—far less than what they expect in return. Taking things for free isn't just a bad habit; it also shrinks one's character, revealing a poverty of honesty, generosity, and self-respect. However, if certain things come to you naturally, without seeking them, it can be considered a stroke of good luck or even karmic rewards. Otherwise, avoid taking things for free. If you constantly seek free benefits, you are writing a destiny of lack for yourself. Also, do not try to extract more for free from anyone whether it's their resources, effort, advice, or time. Understand that all of these have value, and constantly exploiting others corrupts one's character.

If you wish to avoid or end money karma, the habit of expecting free favours, taking more than you give, and failing to reciprocate must stop. This behaviour creates karma that blocks prosperity, often leading to financial hurdles in life. The habit of taking the maximum from someone for free, without returning anything, is the purest form of greed. And greed is rooted in ego. It returns with serious karmic consequences, often manifesting as financial obstacles or an inability to sustain prosperity. Prosperity remains with those who choose to be generous. It eludes those who take excessively while giving little or nothing in return.

So, be careful about accepting free favours. You never know when this habit could turn into a deep-rooted tendency of greed.

In summary, good money karma includes:

a) Not skipping your share of the bill when out with friends.

b) Generously tipping support staff—servers in restaurants, janitors in public places, neighbourhood cleaners, home staff—and rewarding them for their efforts.

c) Donating to causes that benefit the underprivileged, handicapped, elderly, and those in need.

d) Supporting welfare initiatives in whatever way you can.

Remember, all that you give finds its way back to you. Giving is living with a generous heart that spreads joy and positivity. It is an elevated state of being that attracts abundance in all aspects of life.

4. Feel Rich

Always feel grateful for what you have. Appreciate any amount of money that you make. Don't complain, don't feel scarcity, and don't dwell on deprivation. Instead, feel rich with the resources in hand. Because how you feel about your money is the energy you give to it, and that's the kind of wealth you attract.

It is not how you think but how you feel about your financial status that matters. If you feel rich even with limited resources, your energy remains well-aligned. You give positivity to money and show it respect, which helps you do better and dissolves any negativity related to money. Remember, gratitude is a powerful energy. But a truly grateful person remains in touch with gratitude despite life's inconsistencies. Only then does gratitude transform into character. Furthermore, when gratitude is unconditional—not dependent on monetary status—it attracts the correct inflow of money.

So, when we remain grateful for all that we have, without tying that feeling to how much we possess, gratitude becomes a spiritual practice. It also becomes a virtue that helps us vibrate at a higher frequency, which is the aim of any spiritual practice. And from such a state, we are able to dissolve past money karma and attract prosperity into our lives. After all, our frequency must match for prosperity to stay aligned with our life.

Feeling rich also means not comparing one's status with that of others who are labelled rich. Such comparisons can invoke jealousy, lowering our frequency and reducing our chances of attracting the right financial results. In fact, they can also create a karmic response to money, as they border on greed

5. Invest in Hard Work

Work hard to earn your money. Don't take the easy way out. Remember, both your intention and effort must remain equally pure for prosperity to grace your life. Hard work also reflects a positive tendency to create wealth. It demonstrates sincerity and a positive state of being—both essential for dissolving money karma.

So, work hard and earn money the right way, do not cut corners. Do not resist hard work or complain about it, as hard work also helps burn past karma. It reflects good intention and the humility to do what is required. In fact, such a mindset creates true value for money. Not only is it ideal for one's professional life, but even outside one's profession, a hardworking person has a greater chance of succeeding. Their energy remains unblocked due to the absence of resistance, allowing them to eventually attract the rewards of their sincerity. And even if karmic reasons delay these rewards, they are never denied.

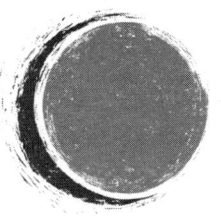

25

Health Karma

Our ego-led ignorance often makes us forget that our body is precious. It is our vehicle to explore the world of forms. But when we become excessively involved in worldly affairs and neglect our physical well-being, we create karma of the worst kind—health karma—and it returns as disease or physical disorder.

Health karma is a complex aspect, and it manifests in different ways for different reasons. One of these is as payback for neglecting our own physical well-being or for the harm we may have caused to the health of others. This can happen through:

1. Lack of work-life balance.
2. Workaholism.
3. Lack of exercise or physical activity and a sedentary lifestyle.
4. Consumption of unhealthy foods.
5. Feeding unhealthy food to others.

6. Malpractices in the field of healthcare and medicine.
7. Engaging in activities that harm the environment.

Thus, it is not just our own health that matters. When we participate in practices that damage others' health, karma returns in some form of bodily suffering. This cycle of cause and effect is deeply intertwined with our awareness—or lack thereof—of how our actions impact both ourselves and others. The lack of awareness is often due to ego, as ego either loves to live in denial or not care for the greater good.

So, once again, our ego plays a decisive role. Ego means ignorance, and we can remain ignorant of our own physical well-being or that of others for various reasons stemming from ego. For instance, excessive ambition and greed for endless material growth can lead us to neglect exercise, healthy eating, timely meals, and proper sleep. Or we may unknowingly make money through businesses or professions that affect people's diet and health, such as those connected to the food industry, medicine, or pharmaceuticals.

Health karma can also accumulate when we engage in professions or activities that harm the environment and, in turn, impact public health, especially when we ignore eco-friendly practices. Industries such as energy, construction, fashion, transportation, and even agriculture contribute to environmental damage in different ways. If we choose to operate in ways that harm the environment, being part of any of these sectors carries karmic consequences.

Therefore, in understanding health karma, people working in industries that affect public health must be extra cautious. They need to ensure their services and practices do not compromise people's well-being.

Any negligence or unethical behaviour—whether in the food business, medical services, or pharmaceuticals—can lead to serious karmic implications. Unethical practices include offering substandard services, exploiting people during medical procedures, overcharging patients, or failing in one's duties as a medical practitioner due to carelessness or deceit.

Mental health issues can also unknowingly create karma with the body. This aspect, linked to the ego, is often caused by overthinking. When the ego generates internal imbalances through continuous mental noise, or when we live in ego-driven fear, we become victims of our own thoughts and emotions. This triggers the release of cortisol, a stress hormone, which can harm our health in the long run.

Let us explore this aspect further.

Mind and Health

Disease can also be seen as an acute disturbance in one's mental state. Since the body vibrates at the frequency of our thoughts and feelings, it attracts all that aligns with those vibrations. When inner peace and stillness are absent, this imbalance can give rise to physical illness. Therefore, mental health must be prioritised if one wants to remain karma-free. However, in today's world, the rise of incessant thinking has led to a sharp increase in mental disorders. We don't even realise when our conscious behaviour takes a backseat to unconscious mind patterns, allowing mental noise to create unnecessary stress, doubt, worry, anxiety, and fear. Some of us find silence awkward, uncomfortable, or even eerie. Others overanalyse situations and people to the point of thinking unnecessarily, thinking negatively, and presuming things that may never happen or may not be true at all. There is also significant content consumption contributing to internal noise, thanks to social media and the internet.

It is important to note here that there are serious karmic implications for those whose minds are perpetually in overdrive. We often assume that karma is only built through interactions with others, but the most difficult karma we create is with our own mental state. This karma arises from abusing the mind with relentless noise and failing to give it rest and positivity. The karmic payback for this can manifest as situations where we are left with no choice but to rest the mind such as being born with mental disabilities, developing old-age senility, or suffering from memory loss. All of these can result from a lifetime of overthinking and the constant voice in one's head. Therefore, it is important to think less, to practice inner silence, and, most importantly, to live with an awareness of the self and one's thoughts. Otherwise, we continue building karma with the body—a karma that will eventually return as disease or physical disorder.

Another important aspect to consider is that leaving the physical body through death does not automatically dissolve health karma caused by mental imbalances. People sometimes go to the extent of ending their lives, believing their problems will end with death but that is not true. The tendencies of the soul remain unchanged for a large part of its journey. Even after death, the soul carries these tendencies into its next form, continuing to vibrate at the same frequency. Thus, if someone struggles with poor mental health, anxiety, fear, or anger, nothing changes unless the soul takes charge of its mental well-being and works to dissolve these tendencies.

Nature and Health

Another perspective on health karma is based on our interaction with the natural environment. Since nature is our source of energy, physical wellness, and peace of mind, we take a lot from it. Hence, how we treat nature has consequences.

It is also true that when we have damaged or destroyed nature in our past lives—or even in the present life—we can suffer from negative health karma. This is because destroying nature amounts to disturbing the elements (air, water, earth, sky, and fire). Since our body is made of these elements, when we disrupt our natural surroundings or act irresponsibly in maintaining their purity, we take on health karma. Even a dying tree transfers its prana (life force or energy) to its immediate environment. So, imagine what a healthy, living tree can do for us— how much it can energise and empower us! That is why cutting down trees and hills depletes the prana shakti or life force from our surroundings, adversely affecting our own health and the health of others—a sure way to build health karma.

Thus, to stop creating or perpetuating health-related karma, we need to focus not just on fitness, a healthy lifestyle, nutrition, mental health, and sleep, but also on the following:

1. Serve Nature

We must respect and serve nature which includes caring for plants, trees, animals, birds, water bodies, and land. By doing so, we balance the energy of the elements and create healthy resources for our own body, which is composed of these five elements. Invoking the positive energy of nature also helps expedite karmic settlement, fostering inner harmony and nourishing our mental and physical health.

Additionally, building a greener planet starts with small efforts: growing a home garden, planting trees, disposing of trash responsibly, cleaning up our pet's waste, protecting water bodies from contamination, conserving energy, minimising plastic use, and more. These efforts matter because we don't just build karma with our bodies, we also build karma with the planet. And this karma, in turn, disrupts both the planet's energy balance and our own. Hence it is important to act with awareness and responsibility toward the environment, ensuring that our choices contribute to harmony rather than harm.

2. Make Clean Money

One of the major causes of health karma is dirty money. If the energy behind wealth accumulation is negative, it invites disease. Negative energy in this context refers to making money through greed, unethical or unlawful practices, shortcuts, tax evasion, and similar means. Earning money through such methods not only weakens one's soul power and strengthens the ego but also creates karmic bondage that affects the entire family living off that money.

We need to understand that money, in itself, has no inherent energy. The energy associated with it comes from how it is earned and how it is used. When money is made through ego-driven tendencies or spent to satisfy the ego, it generates negative energy in one's life—an energy that can manifest as disease or conflict.

3. Offer Medical Help

An effective way to counter health karma is charity. If someone is facing health issues, charity can help bring relief. This is highly effective. Moreover, it does not matter how much one gives; what matters is consistency. Regularly aiding someone in need by covering medical procedures, procuring medicines, or donating to authentic services that support healthcare for the underprivileged can help dissolve one's own karma. However, while charity can provide some relief, it may not entirely erase past negligence, as some karmic payback may still need to be settled through enduring a health battle. That said, charity can be particularly effective in dissolving karma linked to diseases where the diagnosis is unclear or the prognosis remains challenging. Since charitable giving ensures that one's money is used for a noble cause, it not only purifies wealth but also helps resolve past karma where one may have been negligent toward the health of others in various ways.

If financial charity is difficult, one can still contribute by volunteering part-time to support healthcare services. Volunteering is equally valuable in creating good karma and replacing self-centred, ego-driven behaviour with humility and compassion—qualities that connect us to our higher self.

4. Altering Mindset

If you are facing a health crisis, it is crucial not to dwell on the problem mentally. A victim mindset—constantly thinking and talking about one's illness—keeps one in a low-frequency energy field, which not only sustains disease but also hinders spiritual growth.

Remember, if the spirit is strong, even the most challenging illness can be overcome. But when energy remains heavy and blocked with fear, emotional pain, anger, or anxiety, both healing and karmic resolution become difficult. Such tendencies allow the ego to dominate, disempowering the spirit. And when the spirit is weak, the body struggles to heal. Therefore, working on your energy is most important.

Some ways to strengthen and uplift your energy include:

- Positive self-talk.
- Acceptance of what is and eliminating any inner resistance to one's health condition, which helps quiet mental noise.
- Fewer thoughts or discussions about the illness or treatments.
- A less emotional, more practical approach.
- Shifting focus to activities that promote inner stillness, positivity, and calm.

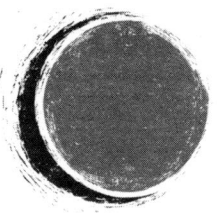

26

Personal Karma

It is true that negative karma isn't always a result of our interactions with others. How we interact with ourselves, how responsible we are for our own peace and well-being, how much we care for our own sanity, and how we live this life in the present moment all contribute to either adding to or dissolving our karmic burden. This is known as personal karma. Let's explore this in greater detail.

Most of the time, karma is simply the lens through which our soul personality is being observed for necessary transformation. This means we also have karmic debts toward the self, which include:

1. Dissolving our ego.
2. Rebuilding our faith in ourselves.
3. Regaining our peace of mind.
4. Restoring our higher self.

A few important questions to reflect on are: How does one recognise when personal karma is playing a dominant role? And how does one know when their primary karmic debt is self-work?

The first sign is having a small number of people to interact with. This doesn't mean one is less fortunate; it simply means more time for oneself. Time to introspect, gain wisdom, reflect, and focus on becoming a better version of oneself. The second sign is a sense of detachment from worldly concerns and aspirations. This may manifest as a disconnect from conventional jobs, career paths, or even relationships. This happens because, at certain points in our journey, self-work becomes the primary focus. Some embark on this path by choice, while others are pushed into it by disenchantment with mundane life. This may be because one's higher purpose is to focus inward to nurture, understand, and transform the self. As a result, relationships or typical routines may lead to disillusionment or push one into solitude. At this stage of evolution, some may opt for singlehood, some may choose an unconventional career that allows them more time for self-reflection, while others may consider early retirement. Any such disillusionment or isolation ultimately serves a purpose—it facilitates self-work for one's own growth.

Let us understand this through a few examples.

- **Example 1**

    If someone is a workaholic, their work may not be their passion but an obsession. A workaholic is deeply insecure and has low self-esteem. They seek to gain self-confidence through their work but fail to realise that, in doing so, they tend to destroy themselves because anything in excess is unhealthy. And rather than strengthening their self-esteem, it only weakens it further.

As their personal karma plays out, there will come a point in their work life when they may either lose their job or start feeling disenchanted or may not achieve the desired results in their field, leading to frustration. This could be a part of their personal karma, where a sense of withdrawal and detachment—integral to one's evolutionary journey—guides them toward a different area of work. This karmic shift may encourage them to slow down, directing them toward work that allows time and space to reconnect with their deeper self and heal the aspects of their personality damaged by their ego. Alternatively, they may be forced to take a break due to extreme exhaustion or even health issues. And while this may come as a rude awakening, it is how personal karma draws them toward fulfilling their duty to the self. This is not to say that all disenchantment stems solely from a need for growth; it can also arise due to major karmic debts. However, even then, when one is pushed toward a solitary path or feels disconnected despite an active work life or relationships, the larger reason is often one's higher mandate: the need to grow and evolve as a being. This growth cannot be achieved unless one shifts significant focus toward the self and starts living and operating through a stronger relationship with the self.

Furthermore, as much as we may believe that relationships are essential for growth and fulfilment, truly successful and karma-free relationships require first achieving absolute harmony within ourselves. We must develop the best possible relationship with the self. Without this, we are bound to encounter pain, hurt, struggle, suffering, and stress in our interactions with others, becoming further entangled in karmic debts.

Thus, when the time comes, it is important to rebuild the self. For this, we either choose a more detached life, or our experiences with others push us in the direction where emotional and spiritual growth awaits us. Either way, when we truly need it— or when our soul has exhausted its major energies and requires renewal—a solitary life becomes the cure. And leading such a life while making the most of the time at hand is, in itself, personal karma.

- **Example 2**
  You may be a good soul, and some people could exploit that by taking -unfair advantage of your goodness. So, how should you deal with such people? Not by immediately disassociating from them, but by showing courage in such relationships and setting boundaries that must be respected. And if they fail to respect these boundaries, you must summon even greater courage to move away from them. This is how

you can be fair to yourself, and this is how you stand up for yourself without giving an egoic reaction.

It is possible that, in the past, you remained stuck in unhealthy relationships for a long time—driven by fear or attachment—without realising that staying in such relationships was unfair to yourself. Now, as part of your personal karma, you may need to either accept these relationships as they are and stop creating suffering by expecting them to be different or choose your sanity by establishing physical and emotional boundaries. Because relationships that destroy your spirit and pull you down eventually make you pay a bigger price for losing yourself. This returns as personal karma, compelling you to learn how to deal with loved ones without attachment or fear and to move away from those who damage your self-esteem and inner peace. While you may be settling a past karmic debt with them, they leave you with an even heavier debt toward the self.

But the most important question is: how does one deal with the isolation or sense of detachment that comes as part of one's personal karma? A few ways to channel aloneness into growth are as follows:

1. By not feeling negative about this state.
2. By not overanalysing the life situation.
3. By understanding that one may be alone because their karmic mandate wants them to reconnect with and reflect on the self.

4. By accepting that there is a karmic past where one may have neglected the self for too long. The present state could be a means to refuel inner peace, silence, and well-being.

5. By keeping the self positively aligned and engaging in creative pursuits to feel inspired and fulfilled.

6. By absorbing wisdom that enhances self-awareness.

The next critical question is: how does one accumulate personal karma? And at what point does it become necessary to address the karma created with the self?

To recognise this, one must cultivate self-awareness and examine the state of their ego. If excessive fear, insecurity, anger, hurt, desires, or attachments dominate one's being, life will present experiences that challenge them to look within. It may manifest through interactions with people who mirror the same tendencies or through growing discomfort with one's own personality. In both cases, life will push one toward self-work.

Additionally, personal karma builds when one resists reality, i.e., when thoughts and feelings reflect a rejection of what is. This manifests in statements like:

- 'I don't want to do this.'
- 'I don't like them.'
- 'I don't like being here.'
- 'I don't like my life.'

Such thinking reflects a deep disregard for life and one's purpose, which requires alignment with certain people, situations, or activities to learn and settle karmic debts. One can never truly evolve or resolve karma while being misaligned with life and its purpose. And so, when things don't happen in life the way we want them to, we are actually being pushed to look within.

Lastly, personal karma is also about fulfilling unfulfilled desires. The goals or dreams we have today are the unfulfilled desires of yesterday. And it is desire that brings us back through rebirth. Desire pushes us to create opportunities that help settle pending karmas. So, wherever there is a balance of karmic debts, we often find ourselves drawn to settle them through our desires. In fact, the pull of karma triggers desires because that is the direction in which we need to invest our energy, time, and purpose. It is, therefore, important to honour our strongest desires. We must not suppress them, for they hold immense scope for spiritual growth. Not only do these desires help us settle karma along the way, but their fulfilment also brings freedom and propels our evolution to a lighter state of being. Because only when we are satiated do we move forward, and desires no longer remain hurdles on our path to enlightenment.

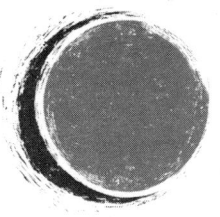

27

Charity: An Effective Way to Burn Karma

'It is our privilege to be allowed to be charitable, for only so can we grow.'
—Swami Vivekananda

The math of the universe operates differently from our own egoic calculations, which endlessly want more, hoard more, gain more, and keep pace with a label-driven world. In the eyes of the universe, or under the karmic law, our capacity to give scores higher than our capacity to earn. Based on this, in life, we are tested on our ability to give, not our ability to accumulate. And when we become givers in every sense—especially when we open our hearts to charity, help others, act selflessly, and sacrifice our own interests for the welfare of others—we score well.

But what does it truly mean to 'give' in the context of karma? Let's take a closer look.

The term 'give' signifies the following:

1. Engaging in anonymous charity.
2. Supporting humanitarian causes or any kind of welfare work, including medical services.
3. Being generous and compassionate towards the less privileged.
4. Paying our dues or taxes with honesty to contribute to society.
5. Volunteering for welfare causes.

Thus, the easiest way to offset the heavy and unsettling energy of karma is by engaging in such high-vibration deeds, especially anonymous charity or any kind of welfare work that supports social, environmental, or underprivileged causes. These actions help burn karma and bring relief. However, if someone is unable to contribute financially, participating in welfare causes as a volunteer is another powerful option.

Charity has two hands: wealth and service, and one can contribute through either. It doesn't have to be something grand or magnanimous. Even a small effort can make someone in distress feel that goodness exists in the world—goodness that understands unspoken words of pain and need and reaches out with care. We need to deliver such goodness. Simply by giving of ourselves— whether through selfless service or financial support for causes that help the less privileged, society, or even the planet—we create positive change. This elevates our character and helps us operate through our spiritual personality, which is the only way all karmic burdens can be dissolved. And charity that benefits the truly needy does the greatest karmic cleansing for the doer, as it reflects humility, which is the opposite of the ego.

We can also say that true charity is our higher self in action. It helps us rise above the frequency of karma. Through our selfless contributions to the well-being of others, we create positive karma, bringing meaningful change to the lives of the helpless and needy. This positivity is extremely powerful in neutralising negative karma from the past. After all, negativity can only be countered with its opposite energy. And when positivity is generated not just through our actions but also through our intentions and tendencies, it dissolves negativity in our lives much faster. This is why charity is so effective in easing the karmic burden.

True charity is also a way to earn blessings (positive energy)—blessings through the good we do, the timely help we give to someone in dire need, and the compassion we transform into acts of kindness carried out in complete anonymity. The most powerful blessings are earned when we help the underprivileged, especially those who do menial work for survival, those who are disabled, elderly, or unable to support themselves, and those with little means to endure tough times, whether due to a medical emergency, job loss, or any misfortune that derails life and leaves them helpless in their hour of need.

Such blessings are important because they help remove hurdles from our own lives. The essence of this truth is beautifully encapsulated in the words of the great Indian spiritual teacher and yogi, Swami Vivekananda: 'Do not stand on a high pedestal and take five cents in your hand and say, "Here, my poor man," but be grateful that the poor man is there, so that by making a gift to him you are able to help yourself. It is not the receiver that is blessed, but it is the giver. Be thankful that you are allowed to exercise your power of benevolence and mercy in the world, and thus become pure and perfect.'

The truth is, when we help someone in need, we help ourselves. Our charity or selfless service is more a favour to ourselves than to others. For we need blessings to strengthen us and remove blockages from our own life path. We need blessings to cultivate more positivity, which helps us become better versions of ourselves. How else do we counter our own negativity or hardened ego? For it isn't prayers but the power of blessings that protects us, helps us, and enables us to rise above our own negativity. So, the good we do for others blesses us. The seeds of our goodness become the flowers in our own garden as karma isn't only about punishment; it is also about rewards. And our little acts of goodness always return, bringing reasons for our own happiness.

Therefore, the help or blessing that comes our way at the most crucial time, when we least expect it, is something we planted through the secret good we once did for someone in dire need. This is how powerful the law of cause and effect is. Whatever help reaches us when we are at a sensitive juncture, whatever rescues us in a moment of extreme need is our own doing. Some good deed of the past, something done in secret to help someone in a similar situation, returns to comfort us in our exact moment of need or even to save us from something negative. Hence, we must always invest in doing secret good.

What No One Told You About Charity

An extremely important aspect of charity is the beneficiary. When you do something for people you know—whether loved ones, relatives, friends, acquaintances, staff, or anyone who personally seeks your help—it is not considered charity. It is simply a karmic engagement due to a past debt. What you share with them is a karmic account. As we have previously covered, there has been a transaction or energy exchange with these souls in previous lifetimes, which is why they are connected to you—whether closely or remotely—in this life. Hence, if they come seeking your help, or if you feel compelled to assist them in any way, it is a karmic payback, not charity. In other words, there is a past connection between you and them; otherwise, they wouldn't be seeking help from you, nor would you feel the urge to provide for them. Your help to them is an effort to close a pending karmic debt. It is what you owe them.

Therefore, do not mistake what you do for people familiar to you (even remotely) or for those who personally seek your help as charity. True charity—the kind that dissolves a greater karmic burden—happens in anonymity, where the giver does not know the receiver, and the receiver has no clue about the source of the help they receive. It also occurs when one volunteers for charitable causes without personal gain, interest, or attachment. Thus, charity that is truly effective in dissolving karma follows these principles:

- It is anonymous.
- It is given to those we have never known.
- It aids those from whom we expect nothing, not even appreciation or support.
- It is directed toward people or causes that do not directly approach us for help.
- It is done without seeking recognition, publicity, or credit.

I would like to conclude this chapter with the following words from the Holy Bible, which perfectly capture the essence of true charity: 'So, when you give to the needy, do not sound a trumpet before you, as the hypocrites do . . . But when you give to the needy, do not let your left hand know what your right hand is doing.'

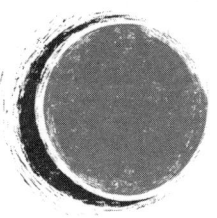

28

Karma: Myth and Truth

'There are certain mechanical features in the law of karma that can be skilfully adjusted by the fingers of wisdom.'

—**Sri Yukteshwar Giri**

Our energy is the quality of our inner state, which determines the nature of our interaction with life. Because how we are is how we feel. How we feel is how we are perceived—it is our vibe, and others sense it. Ultimately, how we are is how we live, and how we live results in what we accumulate as deeds and consequences. So, our energy—our inner state—determines the quality of karmic recording on our soul memory. Unless this energy vibrates at a higher frequency, our inner state cannot remain in order, and we cannot prevent ourselves from accumulating unwanted karma.

Therefore, the beginning of the end of karma starts with us. To work through our karmas, we first need to work on ourselves. Only when we drop the heaviness caused by egoic thoughts, emotions, and behaviours does the power of life flow through us. Otherwise, karmic settlement can become a tiresome journey, stretching across many lifetimes with the same set of souls, events, and experiences that we find challenging. And just as relationships don't last when people's frequencies don't match, negativity also exits one's life when one rises above its frequency. To understand this, one needs to relate to karma through wisdom. Our karmic balances can be offset only by living that wisdom.

Myth: Karma Can Be Corrected Through External Practices

In Eastern cultures, it is popularly believed that meditation, chanting, and even certain rituals and remedies help dissolve karma. However, this is not how it works. Remedies and rituals, in the rarest cases, may help only when they involve some form of penance. Even then, they work only if approached with humility and without treating them as transactions, expecting something in return. For instance, if someone destroyed a religious structure in a past life or plundered a holy place, karma may return as the responsibility to construct a holy place and maintain its sanctity. This serves as both a remedy and a ritual—but as penance. The same principle applies to anything that was destroyed in such a manner, whether forests, buildings, land, or water bodies.

If the destruction caused large-scale harm to human lives, other living beings, or nature, the person may need to spend their lifetime working for the peace, progress, protection, and welfare of large communities or the environment. They may find themselves in professions such as the army, police, firefighting, medicine, environmentalism, or humanitarian work. In all such cases, people return to repair the damage through constructive action and must serve with utmost diligence and humility.

The key to ending karma is to act selflessly, with an elevated consciousness. Rituals and remedies are not the answer unless they involve the restoration of something physical. If there is ego—manifesting as fear, a desire to gain something, or an attempt to avoid suffering—then rituals and remedies only complicate karma, as they corrupt one's intention. Further, practices like prayer, meditation, and chanting do create an environment for change, but even then, they are only effective when pursued with humility, selfless intentions, and an understanding that much more is required to end karma.

The fact is that some people may meditate or chant for a lifetime, yet nothing changes in their behaviour, or if changes do occur, they remain temporary. True liberation from karma comes only by embodying spiritual traits in our behaviour, which requires far more than meditation or chanting. It is only by interacting with life through high-frequency, high-vibration thoughts, feelings, and actions that we achieve freedom from karmic debts.

Subjects like Vedic astrology, a science based on a soul's karmic trajectory and spiritual evolution, offer deeper insights into what a soul needs to correct and help identify karmic mandates through planetary combinations. Psychology, through past-life regression therapies, has revealed past faults to countless individuals, showing how their previous actions bear consequences in the present. In both disciplines, the real solution lies in course correction and behavioural shifts. Additionally, conscious effort, self-awareness, and the right use of free will are necessary to correct past mistakes.

Truth: Karma is Also a Healing Agent

The end of karma is also a form of healing. We encounter karma to heal, and life itself is designed to challenge and elevate us. Its purpose is to build our inner resources and strength, and its course is shaped by our inner state.

At times, karmic experiences may leave us feeling lost and confused. But this is temporary, as no arrangement in life is eternal; it is purely consequential. This applies to karmic experiences as well, for by the end of them, one is bound to feel renewed, awakened, and closer to their higher self, or in other words, healed. Healing occurs when karmic accounts close, debts are settled, the weight is lifted from the soul, and past recordings no longer bind us. Healing happens when we realign with our higher self and shed the ego. However, any karmic experience must first shatter illusions, break conditioning, and knock down the ego. For these very reasons, such experiences can be deeply unsettling. Yet, without them, we would never truly know how far we have come in life.

Karma is the bridge between our ignorant and awakened self. Within our karmic debts lies the immense potential for learning—learning that is essential for awakening and bringing a positive shift in our character. Therefore, we endure life's battles for our own sake. And we struggle because of our ego. The enemy is always within. Our enemy is the ego. And our purpose in life is to dissolve it.

The experience of karma is meant to correct what needs to be corrected. It is an opportunity to end the play of the ego, which leads to healing. But the ego resists, and so karma creates suffering, especially when one resists introspection and self-improvement or fails to break unhealthy habits, conditioning, and behavioural patterns.

Our darkest times are not when we face extreme karmic challenges but when we fail to let such challenges bring out our inner strength—when we refuse to discover more about life or learn something deeper. Our darkest times are when we succumb to misery and pain. Therefore, if you are someone with a challenging life, consider it an opportunity to settle more karmic debts and free yourself. In this freedom lies your healing. Such a life will push you to ask the necessary questions about everything, including yourself. It will lead you to deeper reflection. And if you can establish the link between who you are and what you are facing, and work towards becoming a better person, karma will leave you healed and mature, not scarred or disillusioned.

Yet, the journey from suffering to transformation is akin to a chrysalis becoming a butterfly. Despite the suffering and pain, the chrysalis eventually leaves its egoic cocoon and spreads its wings to experience freedom—the freedom that allows it to truly embrace the joy of living. The transition may be painful, but only by daring to transform can the chrysalis achieve liberation.

Nature has its own beautiful way of demonstrating the loss of ego—letting go of its baggage to emerge lighter. A chrysalis must use all its strength to break open the cocoon and take flight as a butterfly. Another example is that of a snake. A snake cannot continue to grow without shedding its skin. When it is ready to shed, it becomes slow and sluggish. The skin doesn't just fall off; the snake must scrape itself against hard surfaces, often wriggling between sharp edges of rocks, for the skin to peel away. Though the shedding is harsh and painful, the snake emerges energetic and vibrant, with brand new skin underneath. Interestingly, the snake is not taught how to shed its skin. Nature itself has embedded this intelligence to grow and evolve within it. Humans, too, possess this innate intelligence, but unfortunately, it is buried under layers of ego.

So, karma serves a dual purpose. It brings situations that help ease the burden of your debts, which may cause temporary suffering, but this also creates room for awakening and the loss of ego. Eventually, you transform and heal. Because what hits you hard is also meant to awaken you. It is meant to reveal reality and shake you out of conditioned behavioural patterns dictated by the ego—patterns that deplete soul power and cause inner turmoil. And when we release them, we heal. Thus, one could say that karma does not merely punish or reward—it also heals. The pain of karma serves a higher purpose, for in overcoming pain lies the triumph of the spirit. Pain always carries a precious lesson vital to transformation and healing. Without pain, no one dissolves karmic debts, matures, or grows as a person. Pain is not just a healer; it is also a teacher as it helps us evolve into a higher being. And not only does pain release the soul from major karmic debts, it also opens the doors to newer, happier possibilities, provided one does not remain trapped in the experience of pain through emotions and memory, thereby creating further suffering.

One of the most important aspects of attaining wisdom and maturity through a karmic experience is spiritual growth. And karma only ends with our growth. Therefore, not even death can end a karmic debt unless the necessary lessons have been learnt, and the soul attains maturity through the experience. Death can only bring closure to one chapter of a specific karma. But karma itself dissolves only when a soul evolves and rises above its frequency.

Though when one faces karmic challenges, suffers, but learns nothing—when they refuse to work on themselves and die carrying inner complexities and a hardened ego—they will have to return to more challenging lifetimes. In those lifetimes, intense suffering may finally break the ego, forcing the necessary transformation to take place. But when we use free will and perceive life through wisdom, we can close past accounts much faster and without unnecessary suffering. So, if you do good to others and they neither appreciate nor reciprocate your kindness, you must use free will to prevent an adverse reaction and remain humble in your goodness. Because your goodness does more than cleanse dark karmic recordings from your soul—it brightens your aura. And it always comes back full circle.

Your goodness serves you. Life is never about other people; they are merely facilitators on your path. Your goodness is the real goal. It is how your higher self is reinstated. It is also how you heal and end karma.

To heal, the three primary areas of focus must be our feelings, thoughts, and behaviour. Harnessing their collective power to realign with our higher self is the only way we end karma.

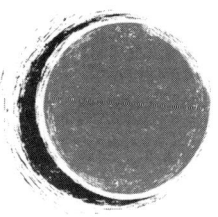

29

Our Feelings and Karma

As human beings, we rely more on our feelings and respond to life through them. Our feelings carry the energy of our emotions, and it is this energy that attracts our experience of life. Since our feelings control us, we become the way we feel. In other words, our feelings also determine our experience of life. When we feel positive, we create positivity, which is reflected in our vibe and energy. And when we feel negative, we create negativity, which then becomes the quality of our own energy. We are, therefore, what we feel deep within.

Thus, the 'secret' is not the thought; the true secret is the feeling behind that thought. We attract everything that vibrates at the frequency of our feelings. This is why affirmations, despite their immense popularity, sometimes don't work, especially when they come from a feeling of lack or subtle desire. While our words may say one thing, our energy the feeling behind those words—reflects something else. And it is energy—not just our words—that shapes our reality. This means that for an affirmation to be effective, one must genuinely connect with it and align their feelings with its essence. That is the true power of feelings.

Additionally, our feelings play a crucial role in shaping our karma. They can attract karma, keep us trapped in karma, or free us from karma. This is because the thread of karma keeps us tied to people primarily through our feelings, and until we learn to cut or transform those negatively charged feelings, we remain trapped in karma. Let us understand how.

Since karma works through our intentions, the nature of our intentions determines our karma. And intention is shaped by what we feel while performing an action, i.e., it stems from our tendency. So, if we do something good for someone out of pressure, compulsion, obligation, or a desire for acknowledgement, appreciation, or personal gain, the intention becomes impure because the tendency is backed by ego. Similarly, if we do something good but do not feel good about it, or if our good deed is merely to end karma, then in all such cases, our actions won't be of much help. Instead, karma is likely to tighten its grip on us rather than set us free.

Put simply, the deep-rooted feeling behind an action determines whether we accumulate negative karma or dissolve a karmic debt. If the intention or feeling behind our deeds is pure, selfless, and detached from emotional gratification, we remain debt-free. If it is free from ego, attachment, greed, or desire, it does not create a negative karmic connection. This is because pure feelings generate good vibes and positive energy, raising our frequency and helping us rise above the low-energy field of a negative karmic connection. They also help others feel good about us, which is essential to breaking the cycle of karma and shifting relationships or life situations into a more positive space.

The power of our feelings also plays a significant role in determining the quality of our relationships. Since others are also influenced by their own feelings, they respond to us based on how they feel about us. Our communication with people is not limited to words or actions; we communicate far more through energy. And it is this energy or vibe that influences people and shapes our experiences. This is why it is important to feel right about others because even when they cannot see or hear us, our energy reaches them through our feelings.

Moreover, we don't have to live with someone to create a karmic account with them. When they occupy a constant place in our feelings—whether through pain, anger, hate, doubt, hurt, fear, jealousy, or attachment—karmic accounts naturally form.

To summarise, the quality of our deeds and their consequences, which amount to karma, depends on how we feel about people, ourselves, and life situations. Therefore, to end karma or create good karma, simply doing good or saying good is not enough. Both must be backed by the right set of feelings because karma begins and ends with our emotions. It results from the energy exchanged through feelings.

So, how can you keep your feelings and emotions balanced and healthy? And how can you use them to resolve past karma while avoiding new karmic entanglements? Here are some key do's and don'ts:

1. Do As You Feel

If something does not align with your feelings, don't say it or do it. This leaves no room for conflict and prevents your energy from becoming confused or heavy. It also protects you from internal conflict and stress, which arise when our feelings contradict our words and actions. Even if you feel negative about something, do not let your words and actions go against that feeling. Express yourself as you feel, or remain silent, but do not say or do anything that contradicts your feelings. Do not try to be nice if you do not genuinely feel that way inside.

The same principle applies to your relationships. You never get entangled in negativity or negative karma when you don't hold back your feelings and instead convey what is necessary—politely but firmly. By doing so, you bring the energy of honesty into a situation, and honesty carries a pure and powerful vibration. It protects you from getting entangled in karma or complicating it.

Furthermore, in relationships, don't just display emotions outwardly; feel them too. Express yourself freely and be forthright when necessary. Say what you mean. This prevents unnecessary tension from building up to toxic levels, especially when difficult emotions are suppressed. One need not be offensive, but one must certainly convey the right thing at the right time for the right outcome. It saves the self from feeling anxious and beaten up and also keeps relationships straightforward and uncomplicated while sending out the right energy.

2. **Stay Light**

In order to stay light, one's feelings need to remain light and positively aligned. And for that, one needs to do what is right. So, talk things out and try to resolve any misunderstandings or misgivings. Offer apologies where necessary and truly feel them. Don't just say sorry for the sake of it. In a situation where we offer an apology but still carry anger and frustration within, the other person neither feels our apology nor forgives us, which has further karmic implications. An apology backed by genuine positive feelings is highly effective in karmic situations and can work wonders in repairing damaged relationships. Also, disagree when necessary. Be vocal about your feelings, but ensure your disagreement is backed by the right emotions. Make sure the feeling is not one of anger or resentment but is instead directed toward creating peace. And do not continue dwelling on the disagreement—do not energise it with more thoughts, feelings, and emotions. Learn to draw a line between external situations and your internal state.

Your feelings do not need to be invested in everything that happens. This is one of the best ways to remain free from karmic entanglements. Additionally, don't always view things solely through the lens of your emotions. Try to see and understand people and situations through wisdom—this helps keep your feelings light. Wisdom is necessary because feelings are often controlled by the ego, whereas wisdom is unbiased and the opposite of the ego.

You must also assess your feelings from time to time. If there is hurt, acknowledge it only up to a point, and then let it go. Don't keep replaying it in your mind, as this only makes your energy heavier. Don't invest your thoughts and emotions in it, as doing so will only intensify the pain. Remember, hurt signifies that you are facing the consequences of past deeds returning as karma. Clinging to hurt means you are not allowing closure to this chapter. So, do not energise any thoughts or emotions that weigh you down. This way, one can untie karmic knots and heal from hurt more easily.

Another way to stay light is to not place too much importance on opinions, whether they come from others or yourself. If you do, you are not living the true purpose of your life, which is to free yourself from the grip of opinions. After all, opinions are just concepts that feed the ego. The more one relies on opinions to define oneself, the heavier the ego becomes. This leads to emotional baggage because where there are opinions, there is also disagreement, and with disagreement comes anger, hurt, attachment, or resentment—all of which serve the ego but disempower the spirit. And karma arises from ego and a disempowered spirit. So, we must not forget that we are here to understand the impermanence of opinions. Opinions shift with people's state of consciousness, their moods, and their loyalties. We need not even take our own opinions about ourselves too seriously, because, in the end, how light we truly are depends on how little we identify with ego-driven concepts.

3. Don't Feel More Than Necessary

We often make the mistake of intensely feeling a life situation and giving it all our energy—so much so that we start believing it to be our whole life and begin seeing ourselves through it. This is when we either become too attached or too disappointed, depending on whether the situation is good or bad. At this point, our ego takes over, and we build our entire existence on false identifications—something that easily destabilises our feelings due to the temporary nature of what we have identified with. As we struggle to cling to this false reality, we become overly possessive, insecure, or even feel like victims, turning the whole situation karmic.

Therefore, as we navigate life, it's important not to feel more than what is necessary. If there is a deep sense of attachment, fear, or insecurity, or if one begins deriving their sense of self from a situation or even a relationship, it is a sign that they are investing their feelings more than required. And since the ego is involved, it becomes an invitation to karma.

To end karma or protect oneself from creating it, the ability to see a situation as just a situation—and not as one's entire life—can be very helpful. Because the situations of our life are not our life. Our life is defined by who we are deep within, how we tackle situations, the experiences we accumulate in the process, and how we respond to life. What helps here is becoming an observer of difficult experiences and witnessing them without judgement or pain. We must cultivate the practice of observing without labelling or judging, without attaching words, meanings, and emotions to a situation or a person. This is how we alter our conditioning and break habitual emotional patterns that create similar kinds of feelings. This is how we create a new and more powerful version of ourselves. And this is how we break the wheel of karma because by being an observer of life, we rise above the frequency of karma.

Particularly in relationships, we must not take people's behaviour toward us to heart, as we harm ourselves by taking others too seriously. Remember, people's responses—even if influenced by past energy exchanges—often have more to do with their inner state, i.e., their fears, insecurities, stress, comfort, peace, and happiness. So, when we interact with people, we are not just dealing with karma but also with personalities shaped over time. Therefore, we must not take things too seriously or create unnecessary emotions that trigger unwanted feelings in response to how people behave with us.

4. Don't Look Away from Reality

We all have a tendency that, when we desperately want things to be how we think they should be rather than how they are, we keep fighting the truth and hoping against hope that things will get better. Yet, deep inside, our feelings remain filled with doubts, questions, worry, anxiety, expectations, and dilemmas. And so, things don't change, partly because there is a complicated past to the present, which we may be unaware of.

There are times when fighting reality serves no purpose, as it only leads to indecisiveness and inaction, amplifying our sense of helplessness. This is unnecessary and unhealthy for our feelings. Therefore, when change does not occur despite our best efforts, struggling with our feelings is futile. Instead, we must live in reality and do our best to make peace with it.

5. Don't Label Anything as Karma

The more you define your situations and relationships as 'karma', the more negativity and karma persist in your life through how you feel about something or someone. A situation or relationship may indeed be karmic, but if you continue to feel the weight of the word 'karma', you continue to vibe at its frequency. And from such a state, you cannot achieve freedom from karma.

To end karma, you must change your reference points at the level of your feelings. This means that for any complicated situation, circumstance, relationship, or life event, you must not attach negativity to your emotions or feel it is all karmic. Doing so only empowers karma. Instead, try to feel neutral or positive. As only from that space can you rise to a higher frequency—one from which you see solutions rather than problems. And it is solutions that end karma.

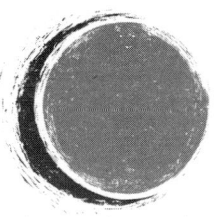

30

Our Thoughts and Karma

'We are what our thoughts have made us; so, take care about what you think. Words are secondary. Thoughts live; they travel far.'

—**Swami Vivekananda**

It is true that we think as we are, and we are as we feel. Our feelings are an expression of our tendencies, and they create thoughts. But what also keeps our feelings or tendencies active is our thoughts. Put simply, we remain the person that we are due to the way we think, and we continue to think the way we feel as our thoughts and feelings share an active relationship, which determines the course of our life. Moreover, since our soul personality or character is built over many lifetimes, it is our tendencies that shape how we think. Tendencies energise thoughts through feelings. So, how we think is just as important as how we feel. And because we think through the mind, how we feel or respond to life, what we create in the process, and the karma we build all result from how we use the mind.

Yet, a point of significance here is that we are not the mind because the mind is merely a human faculty. We use the mind in a certain way to generate thoughts, but we are the user. Therefore, we must not identify the self as the mind. If we take the mind too seriously or identify the self with it, we create problems in our life. In such a state, we become the ego that drives the mind, rather than the awareness that observes it. When we operate through ego, problems inevitably arise, as ego-driven tendencies lead us to think and act in ways that drain our energy. Karma is simply the outcome of these thoughts and actions. And in order to end karma, we must learn to use the mind correctly and not remain its slave due to the misconception that we are the mind or that it is the mind that drives us.

Overidentifying with the mind leads to excessive thinking, which keeps our energy heavy and difficult for others to receive. This mental clutter complicates relationships and life situations, often creating karmic entanglements. Additionally, a restless and overanalytical mind magnifies problems and obscures solutions, turning simple issues into complex struggles. Without clarity and inner peace, we lose the ability to find creative solutions, trapping ourselves in cycles of unnecessary hardship. A constantly overactive mind is drained and powerless, making it more susceptible to anger, frustration, and chaos.

Think of the time when you wake up in the morning after a good night's sleep. Don't you feel recharged and more alive? Doesn't your mind perform better after a nap or a full night's rest? Don't you feel less restless or reactive when your mind has remained silent due to sleep? We all do, and that is because sleep is nature's way of pausing our thinking—something imperative to our mental, physical, and psychological well-being. Additionally, when we meditate or engage in intense physical activities like exercise, running, hiking, cycling, or mountaineering, our mind becomes more focused, and with focus, the speed of our thoughts reduces. That is why we feel rejuvenated after such activities. Some people find driving meditative because it demands focus, reducing unnecessary thoughts and creating a sense of lightness.

So, the problem is not thought itself; it is excessive thinking. Constant thinking is an abuse of the mind. It drains us in ways that not only complicate our behaviour but also affect our energy. As a result, when we interact with others, our energy and behaviour create complications that build karma.

Let us understand how overthinking complicates our interactions with the world.

1. The Karmic Weight of Overthinking

When we overthink—whether about people, situations, the past, present, future, or life in general— our energy vibrates at a lower frequency and becomes heavy and imbalanced. It also overloads the mind and emotions in an unhealthy way. This means there is no space between our thoughts, which reduces our ability to think creatively and blocks energy flow. This is why overanalysing leaves us feeling drained, uninspired, anxious, and stressed.

Overthinking also makes our energy unpleasant to others because no one likes being around heavy energy. This often becomes the cause of karmic relationships since heavy energy leads to a complex mind, which inevitably complicates relationships and life situations. People don't reject us for who we are; they reject us because of how we are. This is also because life isn't easy for anyone, and we are all fighting our own battles. But when someone remains too preoccupied with their mental drama, overloading themselves with thoughts, they add more chaos to the world around them, which, in itself, is karmic. And so, an overthinker is more likely to face serious consequences due to their unconscious behaviour.

2. The Ego's Role in Karmic Entanglement

When we operate excessively at the level of thoughts, without self-awareness or inner stillness, we operate at the level of the ego. This is due to the fact that the ego constantly seeks identification with the world of forms, and it does so through thinking. It makes us think in terms of good and evil, superior and inferior, positive and negative, helpful and harmful—all of which are just labels. Labels lead to judgement and bias, which disrupt our energy by triggering emotions that are often draining and unnecessary.

Judgement and bias also manifest as dislike, anger, hate, criticism, and comparisons—each inherently depleting and vibrating at the frequency of karma. Those who receive such energy from us are not only likely to feel uncomfortable, but depending on their state of consciousness, they may even react in ways that fuel tension in the relationship. The consequences of this are highly karmic. It is also important to realise that even if we do not directly interact with people whom we perceive and assess through negative labels, we still build karma. This is because we contribute negativity to the collective consciousness, disrupting the harmony of other beings.

The key insight here is that karmic complications largely arise due to a lack of spiritual understanding. Unlike the ego, the spirit transcends labels, allowing us to see beyond superficial divisions. When we stop categorising relationships and recognise that we are engaging with souls on a long journey with us, it becomes easier to break negative patterns. And between souls, what truly closes a karmic chapter is a humble reconciliation at the level of thoughts and feelings.

All in all, to end karma and protect ourselves from creating more karmic accounts, we must pay greater attention to our thoughts—they cannot remain unchecked.

Breaking Free from Karmic Entanglements: Harnessing the Mind with Awareness

So far, we have explored how overthinking and overanalysing create complications in life and contribute to karmic entanglements. Now, let's examine how we can harness our thoughts and mind in a way that remains free from karmic consequences.

1. **Use the Mind Intelligently**

   The way you care for your mind determines whether you feel tortured and trapped or light and energised. If you allow the mind to accumulate anxiety, hurt, stress, and worry—whether through poor-quality thoughts, negative information, or excessive overthinking and analysis—you become a prisoner of your own mind. And then you interact unconsciously with the world, creating karma. However, when you prioritise mental well-being and use your mind to generate positivity, you end karma and protect yourself from forming negative ties. By using the mind intelligently, you also contribute positively to the collective consciousness. While it may seem that your mental well-being and inner silence benefit only you, the reality is that they radiate an uplifting energy that influences the world around you.

   To cultivate this intelligence, it is essential to build your inner resources, comfort, and peace. One way to do this is by giving the mind positive nourishment—

feeding it the right information to keep it light and inspired. Additionally, periodically observing your mind naturally slows down excessive thinking, and using your mind consciously—with full awareness of what you are thinking, storing, and habitually telling yourself—ensures that it serves you rather than works against you. Remember, your mind is not a prison; it is a temple. Use it to empower yourself, not to punish yourself.

2. Think Less

Do you think simply thinking right and staying positive is enough to attract what is right? Maybe it is. But is it enough to raise your consciousness and lift you beyond the frequency of karma? Not quite. Because to truly elevate your energy, you must think less.

Fewer thoughts indicate a state of inner peace and stillness—one where you are present, light, and full of vitality. Excessive thinking, even when positive, drains energy and weighs you down. The mind becomes exhausted, creativity diminishes, and energy is wasted on unnecessary mental activity.

Furthermore, an overactive mind—filled with endless thoughts, questions, analysis, and internal chatter—prevents true peace. Doubts, worries, and the relentless need to know, say, or analyse more keep the mind in overdrive. Overthinking is also fuelled by unnecessary assumptions, and more than anything, it is these assumptions that destroy peace and create karma. Peace is lost when we shift from what is to what could be or could have been. It is lost in trying to uncover the 'why' behind everything and in discussing matters beyond our control. True liberation comes not from thinking more, but from thinking less.

Anyone in such a state must give their mind a break by entering a 'no-thought' zone for at least some part of the day. This requires becoming an observer of the mind—experiencing the self as awareness beyond thoughts. This naturally occurs in moments of inner stillness. Stillness means stepping back from the constant stream of thoughts and being fully present in the moment. It involves either watching the mind to disengage from thoughts or becoming completely absorbed in whatever you are doing. True stillness is maintaining awareness behind your thoughts rather than identifying with them.

By thinking less, consciously entering a state of no thought whenever possible, or practising observation of compulsive thinking, you cultivate deep calm. This not only restores balance but also creates a meditative, light state of being. From this elevated energy field, you naturally attract the right experiences, take the right actions, and rise above the frequency of karma.

Pulling back from one's thoughts is particularly effective in the presence of people with whom we've shared a heavy past. This could be family members or anyone we must interact with despite the unrest in the relationship. Such karmic bonds aren't easily dissolved. But what's important in these interactions is to remain attentive to our own mind, not their behaviour.

By paying attention to our thoughts in such moments, we prevent ourselves from succumbing to conditioned emotions that instinctively react negatively—something that happens due to the uneasy energy in the connection. Watching our thoughts precisely in these moments slows down our thinking, which in turn breaks the momentum of reactive feelings.

3. Think Positive

Memory is an important part of the soul because it is memory that guides a soul through lifetimes. And memories or soul recordings are created through experiences and how one deals with them. That is why it is so important to respond with positivity and care, as this creates a memory or recording on the consciousness. In this context, positivity is essential because we don't change the negative in life by trying to fight it. We change it by focusing on what is positive and by reinforcing it, living it, being it, and giving it more space in our lives. This is how we raise our frequency and attract positive solutions to life's problems. But when life's focus is on fighting negativity—resisting it, analysing it, or constantly discussing how to tackle it—too much energy is spent in that direction. This connects us negatively with people and situations, and as a result, we attract more negativity.

Therefore, the way to resolve our problems, which are largely karmic, is not by battling negativity but by increasing positivity. And there is no better way than by thinking positive thoughts. This also helps reduce thinking itself, because the quality of our thoughts determines how much we think. When we think positively, we are peaceful, which naturally quiets the mind. On the contrary, when we think negatively, we feel uncomfortable and anxious, which intensifies our thinking. So, the quality of our thoughts directly influences their quantity.

In order to make positivity the focus of life, one must cultivate positive thoughts and consume uplifting content. This means avoiding gossip, depressive reading, or entertainment that stirs negative emotions. Also, negativity can only be transformed through a positive force. Thus, even when addressing a negative aspect or scenario, it should be evaluated and expressed in a constructive manner to remain free of karmic entanglements. Additionally, consciously conveying perspectives in a positive way helps prevent unnecessary complications.

For instance, there are times when our feelings may hold disapproval, anger, disappointment, or hurt. But if we communicate using thoughtful and dignified words, we can prevent further damage.

Practising this with discipline and consistency not only improves our lives but also helps us rise above negativity. Even thinking positively about a negative person or situation is just as important. This means not clinging to negative feelings for too long. After all, our feelings fuel thoughts. So, when we don't get along with someone yet still silently create positive thoughts for them, we can shift the relationship into a positive orbit and break the wheel of karma.

4. Practice Detachment

Our mental narratives keep us emotionally tied to people, experiences, and life events, often when we should ideally release them because such thoughts are unhealthy for us. At times, they also complicate our karmic connections, making them harder to resolve. Detachment, on the other hand, does the opposite. It is not about anger, hatred, numbness, or disillusionment. Rather, it is the conscious choice to not let our own mind work against us. It means not entertaining thoughts that keep us bound to what we need to let go of. Detachment is refusing to let the energy of our past—connected to people, experiences, and events—dictate our present. Whether this energy stems from a positive or negative past, it strengthens the ego, as the ego relies on the past or future for survival. However, when we free the present from the weight of the past, we create space for something new and wonderful to enter our lives.

Detachment is also one of the most powerful and effective ways to grow spiritually. Unless one is detached, the ego continues to operate and thrive, leading to excessive attachment to people and things. This prevents us from resolving past karma and moving on, entrapping us in recurring patterns across lifetimes.

An important realisation here is that life itself presents situations and experiences that guide us toward understanding the power of detachment. There are times when loved ones leave, and we initially feel loss and grief, but with time, a natural sense of detachment emerges. Similarly, there are moments when we do not receive the affection or support we seek, leading to feelings of heartbreak or betrayal. Yet, in time, we learn not to be affected by it. Such experiences are not meant to encourage resentment but to cultivate detachment. For in the coldness or heaviness of relationships lies an opportunity for spiritual growth. And detachment means that after a point, it simply does not matter. Ultimately, detachment allows us to accept things as they are— not with regret or bias, but with a deep and peaceful acceptance of the present.

5. Silence the Mind

Silence is the space we create between thoughts, essential for breaking free from constant inner noise. It is the ability to observe the mind rather than be consumed by it. The most effective way to cultivate silence is by watching our thoughts. As we do this, they begin to slow down, and with sustained attention, they eventually pause. Even if just for a moment, this pause creates the necessary silence that leads to inner peace, which is therapeutic and empowering.

Silence also serves as a tool for reprogramming consciousness by realigning it with peace—the language of the spirit. Peace allows consciousness to separate from the ego and drop form-based identifications. In peace and silence, subtle impressions that invoke karma lose their power. Since our subconscious stores such impressions, we experience karma when feelings associated with them are reactivated, often through sudden thoughts or emotions tied to past experiences. Such moments can trigger reactions that complicate life and reinforce karmic patterns. The deeper purpose of silence is to disempower these feelings, preventing them from dictating our responses and keeping us bound to unnecessary karmic cycles.

Since silence means no thought—just pure awareness—it is the most powerful way of experiencing life. It is the ability to see oneself as separate from the mind. Silence also helps develop intuition, which is essential for finding solutions that bring closure to past karmic accounts. Since our intuitive sense is far superior to mind-made stories, which complicate things through overthinking and overanalysing, silence helps us discover the right solutions to karmic issues.

When we stop being compulsively led by the mind, we begin to understand life. The key insight here is that the mind is often a trap of the ego, while intuition is the call of our conscience. And we can only tune into intuition when we stop perceiving things solely through the mind's perspective, or in other words, when we become an observer of the mind. This is how stress is prevented from taking over, and how we arrive at the solutions to life's problems.

6. Don't Use Thoughts to Escape What Is

Since most overthinking revolves around the past or the future, living in the present and being fully attentive to what is helps conserve our energy. It retains our positivity and protects us from worry and stress, which can contribute to karmic cycles. Trouble arises when we dwell on the past or obsess over the future, as this misaligns us with life. It creates imbalance and disharmony within, draining our precious energy. And from such a state, we only complicate life and karma. Thus, living in the present moment and doing the best one can is the greatest way to ease karmic burdens.

Unfortunately, our egoic self loves to recall the past, especially when we have suffered. The past provides a strange sense of comfort and an identity rooted in victimhood, which the ego needs to survive. At times, we even use our stories of suffering to prove to the world that we are heroic. But in both cases, it is the need for identity that compels us to keep revisiting the past. And when we recall negative karmic situations, we bring that energy into the present, extending it into the future. Therefore, we must recognise that by constantly talking about or reflecting on past suffering—or even merits—we not only appear weak but also feed the ego, or more precisely, our low sense of self-esteem, which craves some form of identity. The key takeaway here is that wasting energy on the past or future disconnects us from life, which exists only in the present. It also ruins our equation with time. When we resist the present moment, we resist life itself, disrupting our alignment with time and inviting unnecessary complications that lead to negative karma.

To stay in harmony with life and ourselves, our thoughts must remain anchored in the now. The past is merely a memory—we cannot return to it. The future is only anticipation or imagination, and life isn't in anticipation or imagination. Life is in what is happening now, at this moment. Escaping into the past or future is a disregard for time, and since time and life are one, it is a rejection of life itself.

To master life, we must value time. Training our thoughts to stay present allows us to surrender consciously to what is, creating a harmony that grants strength and wisdom. Such wisdom is often the necessary insight or guidance that helps us move past karmic bondage. Remember that while we cannot change the past, we can act in the present to ensure it does not burden our future.

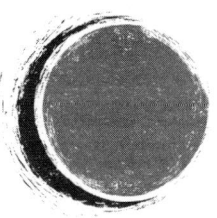

31

Our Behaviour and Karma

'Once the ego has been transcended in soul-consciousness, the realm of karmic law is transcended also. The soul remains forever unaffected, for karmic consequences accrue only to the ego.'

—**Paramhansa Yogananda**

Our higher self is a threat to the ego, as the ego's role starts diminishing once the higher self comes into action. Our higher self is immersed in positive tendencies, and when such tendencies drive our behaviour, we achieve growth and the dissolution of ego. And since our tendencies are the seed of karma, the most powerful and effective way to end karma—and not accumulate more karmic debt—is by choosing to operate through tendencies that empower our behaviour or tendencies that are the opposite of our egoic self. When our character and behaviour are dominated by tendencies of happiness, peace, love, truth, courage, ease, acceptance, kindness, and compassion, our experience of life becomes more pleasant, forming a rock-solid defence against karma. On the other hand, egoic tendencies that activate fear, anger, attachment, judgement, criticism, greed, resentment, and vanity endanger us, tightening our karmic knots.

So, the power lies in our response to life and to past karma, which unfolds through our experiences. The power lies in activating and consistently using the right tendencies aligned with our higher self. Because when it comes to karma, we don't know what we have left behind. We don't understand how it is coming back. But what we do know is that in any given situation, we must keep doing our best—this is the only path to redemption and freedom. We must face the results of past actions with courage and strength, raising our consciousness to a fearless state where we break the wheel of karma.

A good way to cultivate tendencies that empower our spirit and the journey of life is by reflecting them in our behaviour, i.e., by making our behaviour a spiritual practice. The sole purpose of any spiritual practice is to help us align with our spiritual nature, which is our higher self. However, our growth depends entirely on how well we integrate our spiritual nature into material life. Unless we allow our higher self to operate, we cannot grow spiritually, and without spiritual growth, there can be no freedom from karma.

An important point to note here is that spirituality is not about renouncing the world of people and things; it is about renouncing the world of our own ego.

Additionally, life always provides the ideal opportunities for spiritual growth. When we resist this growth, we invite further karmic complexities and continue to create new karmic accounts which make healing and evolution impossible. So, the only way to evolve and rise above the damaging frequency of karma is by allowing our spiritual nature to drive our interactions with the world of forms. When the high-frequency tendencies that define our spiritual nature reflect in our behaviour, a great deal can be resolved.

Let us explore how certain tendencies, when used as a spiritual practice, help us end karma.

1. Peace

Peace is our true nature. It elevates our consciousness, automatically enriching our experience of life and increasing productivity, efficiency, and positivity. A peaceless person is always tired, frustrated, uninspired, bored, angry, critical, dissatisfied, and less efficient. And from such a state, one makes their interactions with the world quite karmic. As souls, we need peace the most as it helps us vibrate at the highest frequency and create the right response to life, which is all it takes to end karma. Without peace, we cannot even begin to resolve karma.

To grow peaceful, one must first learn to create peace, operate in peace, and give peace. The fact is that we do not become peaceful by thinking, reading, or talking about peace. Instead, we become peaceful when we live peacefully with people, life, and situations that threaten our peace. We become peaceful when we create more peace and when we feel it. Moreover, expecting peace from a peaceless world while making no effort to create it—whether through peaceful thoughts, interactions, or actions—is precisely why it remains elusive. The more we cultivate peace, the more it influences others, encouraging them to respond positively. From a place of peace, we can view situations dispassionately and without bias, which weakens negativity. And our peace grows not by fighting negativity but by increasing positivity. Such positivity thrives in inner stillness and silence, in simple acts of letting go. These align us with our higher self and restore peace.

However, with karmic accounts, peace is often elusive. And if one chooses to remain in a situation or with a person karmically connected to them, they must pull back from the mental noise. A noisy mind, regardless of how positively it thinks, has its own limitations. Therefore, creating more silence within—thinking no more than what is necessary for taking action—is your best defence against karma. Also, more often than not, when peace is missing, it signals that a major karmic account may be destined for closure. So, when karmic debts confront us— when people misbehave with us or life gives us what we least expect—if we do not leave our state of peace, we are bound to settle such debts much sooner. This is an empowered response—one that naturally repels or transforms negative energy.

When one finds themselves in situations where, despite trying hard, peace seems impossible, their priority must still be their own peace. Therefore, if things don't work out in a relationship or any life situation, it is better to move away and work towards creating peace. This can only happen by distancing oneself physically from a pursuit or a person and, more importantly, by not keeping one's experience with them energised through thoughts, feelings, and emotions. Because true distancing must first occur at the level of thoughts, feelings, and emotions, only then does one stop fuelling a negative situation or relationship and create the right energy. In doing so, peace gradually returns. This, in turn, creates room for reconciliation or better prospects that bring karma to an end.

A peaceful reconciliation is also possible through letting go. When you let go, you achieve freedom and peace as well as experience a sense of inner lightness and spaciousness. Letting go also creates space for new and positive things or people to enter your life. Your energy attracts them, as you show a readiness to embrace something better. Furthermore, when you let go, you honour life, and in return, it empowers you. It lends you greater maturity, strength, and power. But when you hold on too tightly to anything—whether good or bad—you create attachment and begin to feed the ego. This neither allows you to be at peace nor permits you to grow. It also pushes people away from you because your energy confuses them and causes extreme discomfort. Holding on too tightly also destroys spontaneity and disrupts the flow of life. It attracts more confusion and chaos, keeping you trapped in the ordinary. Your energy becomes heavy, drawing in more of the same. In this way, clinging too tightly creates karmic complexities that linger for a long time. Remember, there is no greater peace and power than what one experiences when one lets go of anything that has held their emotions too tightly for too long. And it is this peace and power that give rise to better things in life.

All in all, our reservoir of peace helps us handle karmic experiences correctly. It allows us to bring closure to anything karmic that would otherwise find extension in anger, unrest, hurt, or other egoic responses. Peace allows us to transform or even break the cycle of karma, which thrives on our habitual tendencies. The more peaceful we become, the less power karma has to sustain itself.

2. Humility

In simple terms, humility is the opposite of the ego. It does not need to hide anything or pretend to be what it is not. And so, when one is humble, one is real and at peace, and there is no room for conflict within, no façade, no mental noise . . . only silence.

Our ego drives us to resist anything that falls short of our expectations, whether through disappointment, anger, criticism, or hurt. Thus, we torture ourselves by expecting what isn't and by keeping ourselves at the mercy of what is beyond our control—something that inevitably makes life hard and painful. But the power of life flows in acceptance, and any form of acceptance arises only from humility.

Humility is a higher form of surrender, i.e., surrendering the desire to control, criticise, and remain in conflict with what is. It is the surrender of the ego, which is ever unwilling to accept things contrary to its expectations.

The primary aim of any karmic experience is also to humble us by making us understand how it feels to be the receiver in a scenario where we were once the giver. Especially in the context of a negative past, the aim is not to punish or hurt us but to help us live with greater awareness of human emotions, understand how fragile and sensitive they are, and recognise the need to handle them with greater care.

Humility lies in understanding that we cannot be too headstrong or opinionated about people or our life choices. In other words, true humility means accepting that we aren't always right and acknowledging the unpredictable nature of life. It also involves not letting the ego interfere with our human connections. Since karmic law states that what we give is what we owe, humility prevents us from seeking credit for our actions and instead allows us to find joy in helping others. The more selfless and humble we are in our giving—or in what we do for someone—the faster our karmic debts dissolve.

Humility nurtures gratitude, which goes beyond simply feeling thankful for the good in life. True gratitude means accepting both the good and the difficult. It is being thankful for what is good and being neutral to what is challenging. This means embracing life as a whole rather than in selective moments. It is about recognising our blessings—not in contrast to someone else's misfortune, which stems from ego, but by cultivating an unconditional appreciation for life, independent of circumstances, situations, or events.

So, the next time you feel grateful because your life seems better in comparison to someone else's, remember that this isn't humility but ego. The ego thrives on unhealthy comparisons. But when we appreciate life itself, without tying our gratitude to what it brings, we align with our higher self. Gratitude then becomes a virtue, raising our vibrational energy to a level where negativity dissolves and the cycle of karma finds closure.

3. Courage

Courage means facing life with dignity and responsibility without rejecting, blaming, or resenting it. Even when we must challenge external circumstances, true courage lies in not wasting energy on anxiety or frustration. It is about taking necessary action while maintaining inner calm, which is always a source of strength.

Courage is an essential virtue because, before we can create the life we desire, we must first find the courage to navigate the life we may not have chosen. This includes facing complicated karma—challenging experiences that may not be easy to endure—but can only be handled through resilience and inner strength. And so, for those engaged in a long struggle against life, resisting what is, or questioning why things aren't changing, why they feel trapped in repetitive cycles, or why they face disappointment and despair, courage is the only way forward. Therefore, even if things are going terribly wrong, one should develop the courage to be at peace with what is. Because when you show the will and the courage to live the life you do not want to live, you not only honour life but also your pending karmas. You rise above the limited mindset of the ego, and in doing so, you settle karma faster by removing the blocks that stand between you and the life you desire.

Courage also means standing on the side of truth, which is never easy. Truth is essential for resolving karma because nothing entangles us more than our inability to see life and ourselves clearly. However, when we find the courage to embrace the truth, we begin to live in alignment with reality—an experience that is both enlightening and empowering. From this state of awareness, we accept karma for what it is and take the necessary steps to settle our debts.

Speaking the truth is equally crucial for karmic closure because unspoken words and suppressed emotions build internal unrest and often cause more harm than the truth itself. They silently drain our energy, creating unnecessary complications, confusion, or negativity in others. That is why expressing the truth is so important.

It is also essential not to remain silent or pretend to agree when, internally, we disagree. Suppressing our truth creates an inner conflict between our energy, words, and actions, only complicating relationships. Courage allows us to speak honestly, to say what we truly mean, and to withhold nothing. It keeps our energy light and our spiritual strength intact, helping us rise above the frequency of karma and resolve past debts. The reality is that it takes courage to live this life—to understand, to give, to trust, to feel, to love, to serve, to dare, to dream, to forgive, to be fair, to do good, to rise from failures, to stay humble in victories, to accept the unexpected, and to survive the storms. Learning to be courageous is the real purpose of life, for courage elevates our consciousness and is a powerful expression of one's higher self.

Finally, here is a small reminder: karmic math isn't meant to torment you; it exists to awaken you and bring you closer to your higher self. And so, you need to understand karma not as a punishment but as a lesson in peace, courage, and humility. Empowered behaviour means all three remain active.

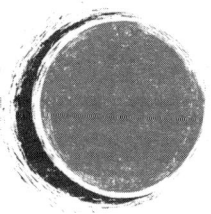

Conclusion

Let us conclude with this powerful truth: Life is simply an experience, a journey of evolving through pending karmas. It ends when our punya (rewards) and prarabdha (debts) have served their purpose of imparting necessary lessons that cultivate depth and spiritual maturity. And the cycle of life continues, where death is merely a transition to another life, another experience, another payback, another lesson, another set of rewards, and an opportunity for further growth.

While a hard life signifies the closure of major karmic debts and a soul moving toward awakening and freedom, accepting each life as an opportunity for spiritual growth—rather than resenting the lessons it brings—helps one achieve its true purpose. Resistance only strengthens unwanted karmic imprints, making life more challenging. Ultimately, we are here to learn and evolve, and everything else, including karma, is just a means to that end.

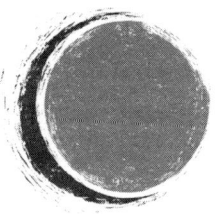

Acknowledgements

While all wisdom comes from the Source, we writers are fortunate to learn on the job. So, in many ways, writing this book has been a humbling experience. While the subject was challenging and putting ideas together intense, I felt guided by positive energy throughout. With the blessings of the masters, I was greatly advantaged and able to accomplish the task. My gratitude to them for their intuitive communication and all the timely help.

This marks my third collaboration with Hay House India, and I am thankful for their continued belief in my work. It is always inspiring to develop a subject that adds value to people's lives. My heartfelt gratitude to Mr Ashok Chopra for providing a platform where writers can connect with like-minded readers and create a meaningful impact. Special thanks to Mr Raghav Khattar for leading the team with dedication and vision, ensuring that important books reach the world. I also appreciate his thoughtfulness in designing the simple yet striking cover of this book.

And since every writer needs a sharp and incisive editor to shape a manuscript into its best form, I am grateful to have found that support in Aditya Jarial. His candid, relevant advice and meticulous attention have elevated this manuscript, and his contribution is deeply valued.

I extend my gratitude to my family—my parents, whose values laid the foundation for my pursuits; my pet Zeus, whose endless affection is a constant source of joy; and my sister Swati, my unwavering supporter and eternal advocate. Your belief in me means the world.

I wouldn't be writing books without the steadfast support of my partner, Manoj. A patient listener to my raw ideas, his encouragement and willingness to help in every possible way have been invaluable. No amount of gratitude is enough for this kind and gentle soul.

Finally, to all those who follow my journey on social media, read my work, and find inspiration in my words—thank you. Wherever you are, your support means everything.

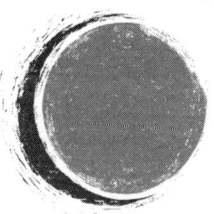

About the Author

Meetu Bisht is a bestselling author driven by a passion for redefining spiritual concepts with depth and originality. Her work emphasises the importance of self-awareness and personal transformation, encouraging readers to explore the self and the world beyond labels and conditioned perspectives. Through her books and social media, Meetu aims to spark spiritual awakening and encourage conscious living.

To explore more of her work, visit **www.meetubisht.com**

CONNECT WITH
HAY HOUSE
ONLINE

🌐 hayhouse.co.uk   **f** @hayhouse

📷 @hayhouseuk   🦋 @hayhouseuk.bsky.social

♪ @hayhouseuk   ▶ @HayHousePresents

Find out all about our latest books & card decks • Be the first to know about exclusive discounts • Interact with our authors in live broadcasts • Celebrate the cycle of the seasons with us • Watch free videos from your favourite authors • Connect with like-minded souls

'The gateways to wisdom and knowledge are always open.'

Louise Hay